HISTORIC WATERWAYS
SCENES

LONDON & SOUTH-EAST ENGLAND

Frontis:
This picture taken in March 1908, from Hammersmith Bridge shows seventeen Thames sailing barges and at least nine lighters. The crane in the foreground is unloading large blocks of ice from a wooden lighter, into a horse and cart.

HISTORIC WATERWAYS SCENES

LONDON
& SOUTH-EAST ENGLAND

Martyn Denney

Moorland Publishing

© M. Denney 1980
First published 1980
Paperback edition 1993

ISBN 0 86190 508 3

Printed in the UK by:
The Cromwell Press Ltd
Broughton Gifford, Wiltshire

Contents

Introduction

The evolution of inland water transport in Britain has spanned many centuries. Just as the axe was a natural progression from the club, so the use of rivers was a natural progression from coastal and esturial shipping. Rivers became natural highways, reaching long silvery fingers to the interior of the land. They had a profound effect on the development of communities and centres of trade. Roads were expensive to construct and costly to maintain; heavy loads often having to wait months until conditions were dry enough — and the roads therefore hard enough for them to be moved. It is of little surprise then, that communities dwelling on the borders of naturally navigable rivers, being at an advantage, attained a higher standard of living and culture than more remote settlements. In Saxon times we can see such places mentioned: Gloucester, Tewkesbury, Bridgnorth and Shrewsbury on the Severn, London and Oxford on the Thames, Ware on the Lee, Rochester on the Medway, Peterborough on the Nene, Lincoln on the Witham, York on the Ouse, Doncaster on the Don, Cambridge on the Cam, Exeter on the Exe, Hereford on the Wye, Chester on the Dee, and many more. In time, these rivers were improved, weirs being built to maintain a depth of water over shallows, and some cuts being made to straighten tortuous sections.

The construction of artificial canals in Britain began with the Fossdyke and Caerdyke during Roman times. The Fossdyke, improved in the twelfth and seventeenth centuries, remains in use today.

Nowadays, it seems inevitable that canals should have been built to connect the major rivers or to serve parts of the country that were away from natural rivers; in the eighteenth century, a catalyst was needed. That catalyst came in 1759 with the partnership of James Brindley, a millwright-turned-engineer, and Francis, 3rd Duke of Bridgewater, in the construction of the Bridgewater Canal from his mines at Worsley to Manchester; and subsequently in 1766 with a number of landowners and industrialists (including Earl Gower, the Earl of Stamford, the Duke of Bridgewater and Josiah Wedgewood) building the Trent and Mersey Canal. What followed was a canal explosion, with nationwide construction continuing until smothered by railway mania.

South-East England followed this basic pattern of development. The Thames has always been navigable, certainly in the lower reaches and possibly in the upper reaches too, likewise, the River Lee. The Danes are reported to have sailed to Hertford in AD894 and we know that they sailed 20 miles north of London to establish a fort in AD896. They are supposed to have made Ware their base and sacked Hertford. Their further progress is reported to have been halted by King Alfred, who stranded their ships in the upper reaches, lowering the levels by dividing the Lee into three channels at King's Weir, Cheshunt, and constructing an embankment and weir known as the Black Wall at the entrance to the Lee from the Thames. This story is supported by the remains of Viking Ships found in the River Beane near Hertford and at Stanstead Abbots.

Later, the Thames featured in another Danish invasion. King Ethelred II, the Saxon, had pawned his kingdom to Canute, and on his death, his son Edmund Ironside was only recognised as monarch by a few faithfuls, including the citizens of London. Canute ruled Wessex, Northumbria and Mercia, leaving Edmund only the City in which to make his stand. However, London was almost invincible, with the Thames blocking the routes from the South. In early 1016, Canute sailed from Southampton to Greenwich, where he set up a fortified camp. Knowing from experience that London was virtually unapproachable, even by water, while London Bridge stood, he planned to outflank it by digging a canal from the river at Rotherhithe, four miles across what is now South London, to rejoin the river at Battersea. Canute completed the canal and used it for some time, until under pressure from Edmund, he was forced to retreat down it to evacuate his men by ship. Canute is also reported to have sailed up the River Effra as far as Brixton. Other tributary creeks and streams leading into the Thames around London were also in use for navigation. The Fleet was used for the carriage of stones for rebuilding St Paul's Cathedral between 1110 and 1133.

To the south, the Eastern River Rother was navigable from Rye, by Appledore and Newenden to Bodiam at least, and was used by the Romans, Saxons and Normans. Further west, the River Arun was partly navigable in 1066, and Arundel is mentioned as a port at the time of the Domesday Book.

As mentioned earlier, the advantages of water-borne transport over the very poor roads of the time were quite distinct, and the development of communities at waterside sites became a noticeable phenomenon even within the mainly agricultural communities of South-East England. During the twelfth, thirteenth, fourteenth and fifteenth centuries, attempts were made by local government and the Church to improve navigation by scouring out river beds on the Thames, Fleet, Lee and Itchen. However, on all rivers the animosity between the navigation and milling interests caused such problems that free navigation was all but unknown. In 1515 Canterbury Corporation obtained an Act of Parliament which enabled them to improve the River Stour between Fordwich and Canterbury, to the same state as that between Fordwich and the sea, and

... to remove all mills and other annoyances on it, insomuch that lighters and boats might be brought to both [Canterbury and Fordwich] alike.

The sixteenth and seventeenth centuries were a period of far greater river improvement. Attempts were made to make the Medway navigable upstream from Maidstone both by local ironmasters and timber growers, and by the Commissioners of Sewers, but these were abortive and had to wait until the Act of 1740. Four successful Acts of Parliament were passed during the seventeenth century for the River Wey (1651), Hampshire Avon (1665), Itchen (1665), and Fleet (1670). The Wey had been used locally for navigation for a considerable time, and in the early seventeenth century various attempts had been made to promote bills to improve parts of the river. The Act of 1651 was promoted by a number of local landowners, led by Sir Richard Weston, the then encumbant of Sutton Place near Guildford. In November 1653, the 15-mile navigation with its thirteen pound locks was completed at a cost of £15,000 and connected Guildford with the Thames at Weybridge. The pound locks constructed were amongst the first in Britain and were of simple design being in many cases turf sided, and little more than a very short piece of river enclosed at either end by a pair of gates. The Navigation was extended in 1760 by 4½ miles and four locks as far as Godalming.

The pound lock is a natural progression from the staunch or flash lock, with its single set of gates, but its invention is attributed to Chiao Wei-Yo, assistant commissioner for transport on a section of the Grand Canal of China in AD983. The first known pound lock in Europe was built at Vreeswijk on the River Lek in Holland in 1373. Both these examples had vertically rising gates; it was Leonardo da Vinci, as engineer to the Duke of Milan who conceived the idea of locks with horizontally swinging mitre gates. The first pound locks in Britain were built on the Exeter Canal between 1564 and 1566, again with vertically rising gates. The first pound lock with mitre gates in Britain is thought to have been constructed at Waltham Abbey on the River Lee in 1580. In 1589 William Vallens described it thus, in his poem *The Tale of Two Swannes*:

Among them all a rare devise they see but newly made
A Waterworke the locke through which the boates of Ware doe passe with Malt.
This locke contains two double doores of wood, within
The same a cisterne all of plancke which only fills
When boates come there to passe by opening of these Mighty doores with sleight.

The River Itchen in the Hampshire Basin appears to have been improved by the Bishop of Winchester at the end of the twelfth century, but deteriorated over the years, so that by the early seventeenth century it

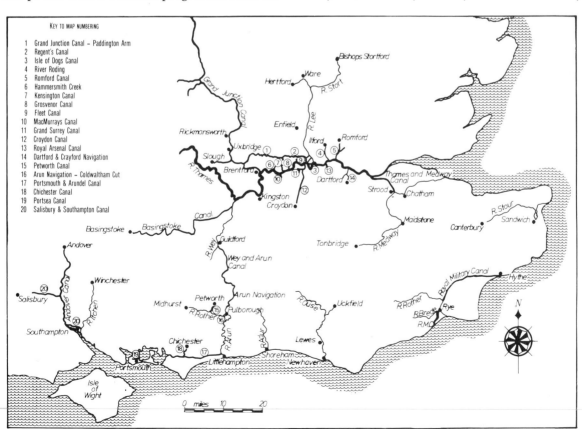

KEY TO MAP NUMBERING

1 Grand Junction Canal – Paddington Arm
2 Regent's Canal
3 Isle of Dogs Canal
4 River Roding
5 Romford Canal
6 Hammersmith Creek
7 Kensington Canal
8 Grosvenor Canal
9 Fleet Canal
10 MacMurrays Canal
11 Grand Surrey Canal
12 Croydon Canal
13 Royal Arsenal Canal
14 Dartford & Crayford Navigation
15 Petworth Canal
16 Arun Navigation – Coldwaltham Cut
17 Portsmouth & Arundel Canal
18 Chichester Canal
19 Portsea Canal
20 Salisbury & Southampton Canal

was in a very poor state. The Act of 1665 enabled a number of named undertakers to rebuild the navigation, but they ran out of time, being forced to apply for several extensions. It was not until 1710 that the navigation was completed to Winchester with locks, cuts and towing paths. Unfortunately, over a period of time, by purchase, transfer and other means, the whole property of the navigation became vested in a Mr Pyott, who charged the tolls he thought fit. In consequence, in 1767 the inhabitants of Winchester promoted an Act to appoint commissioners who would set the tonnage rates. The navigation was $10\frac{5}{8}$ miles long with fifteen locks (twelve turf sided and three masonry) and two single-gated locks, from Woodmill to Winchester.

The Act of 1665 had also authorised the improvement of the Hampshire River Avon from Salisbury to Christchurch, but no work was done until Salisbury Corporation took it upon themselves. A start was made late in 1675 but little was done until they gained outside support in 1677. Apparently barges reached Salisbury in 1684, but tonnage rates and regulations were not issued until 1687.

The last of the seventeenth-century Acts listed was for the River Fleet (or Fleet Canal). It had been navigable with difficulty for centuries, but the whole area was destroyed by the Great Fire of London in 1666. It was inevitable that the Fleet should become a part of the plans for rebuilding the City. The first ideas were fairly simple. At a meeting of the Privy Council held at Berkshire House on 12 March 1667, it was King Charles II who recommended '... that instead of raising Fleete Bridge Six ffoote, it may be raised Nine Foote high, without which Boats will not be able to pass under....'

Evelyn in his *Londinum Redivivum* was rather more ambitious and talked of flood gates and wharves, but it was not until April 1670 that the river Fleet was included in the second Act for rebuilding the City. The Act allowed the river to be deepened for navigation from the Thames to Holbourne Bridge with wharves on either side and specified that:

> ... the sinking and making up of the said ... Fleet Ditch from the channell of the Thames to Holbourne Bridge and the Sasses [locks] and sluces for the better navigation thereon and the raising ... of wharves ... shall be borne and first defrayed by the ... City of London out of the said fourth part of the Imposition to be raised upon Coles ....

The work was put in the hands of Christopher Wren, His Majesty's Surveyor, and Robert Hooke, the Surveyor of New Buildings, who in turn engaged John Bull and Thomas Fitch as contractors. Bull and Fitch quarrelled, and Fitch continued alone. Eventually, work was completed in early 1675 at a cost of about £47,000. Whether or not a lock was built is not clear, our only clue being an order from the City of London Council:

> ... that the Double Sasse according to the Moddell here presented made by [Mr Wren] at the request of the committee be forthwith prepared and fixed by the said Mr Fitch, near such a place about the Rang of the buildings at the end of Blackfryers as shall be determined as about by [Mr Wren]....

The Fleet Canal remained in use until the early 1730s, when trade had dwindled so much that in 1733-4 the section from Fleet Bridge to Holborn Bridge was filled in, to be followed by the lower section to the Thames in the 1760s, when Robert Mylne was building the new Blackfriars Bridge.

The gradual improvement to navigation in the South-East continued through the first six decades of the eighteenth century, with Acts for another four river navigation schemes. First in 1737 came the Act for the $1\frac{3}{4}$-mile Roding navigation from the head of Barking Creek to Ilford Bridge. The scheme was being carried through by Joseph Goodman, but unfortunately he died, and the navigation was eventually completed around 1764 by John Webb.

Various attempts had been made to make the River Medway navigable and in 1664, an Act of Parliament had been passed, granting a number of landowners headed by Lord Muskerry of Summerhill, the right to improve the river, but unfortunately they could not raise the funds. However, on 30 April 1740, an Act was passed forming the Company of Proprietors of the Medway Navigation, and authorising them to make the river navigable from Mistress Edmunds's wharf at Maidstone, to Forest Row, Sussex. The 16-mile navigation with its fourteen locks was opened to Tonbridge on 2 February 1744 at a total cost of £11,419.

In 1766, two Acts of Parliament were passed, for the Lee Navigation and for its tributary the River Stort. The Lee had been the subject of Parliament's Authority several times before, but the Act of 1766 was the most important legislation affecting the navigation up to that time. It authorised the construction of a large number of new locks and lock cuts, which were added to by another Act in 1850. The Stort on the other hand had not been navigable before, despite an abortive Act in 1759 and it took the Act of 1766 to set up Commissioners who succeeded in completing the scheme within three years and one month, to open it on 24 October 1769, 'to the great benefit of Bishops Stortford'.

The period 1778-1830 represented the boom years in South-East England, with both canals and river navigations being constructed and opened.

Chronology of Inland Waterways in South-East England 1778-1830

1778	Basingstoke Canal Act
1785	Arun Navigation Act
1789	Andover Canal Act
1790	Sussex River Ouse Act
	Arun Navigation completed

1791	Western Rother Navigation and Petworth Canal Act
1792	Lower Medway Navigation Act
1793	Grand Junction Canal Act
	Petworth Canal completed
1794	Western Rother Navigation completed
	Andover Canal completed
	Basingstoke Canal completed
1795	Grand Junction Canal, Paddington Arm Act
	Salisbury and Southampton Canal Act
1799	Isle of Dogs Canal Act
1800	Thames and Medway Canal Act
	Petworth Canal disused
1801	Croydon Canal Act
	Grand Surrey Canal Act
	Surrey Iron Railway Act — MacMurray's Canal
	Grand Junction Canal — Paddington Arm opened
1802	Salisbury and Southampton Canal opened as built
1804	Authority for Royal Military Canal
1805	Grand Junction Canal, main line opened from Brentford to Braunston upon completion of Blisworth Tunnel
	Isle of Dogs Canal completed
1806	Royal Military Canal completed
	Salisbury and Southampton Canal disused
1807	River Adur Act
1809	Croydon Canal opened
1810	Grand Surrey Canal opened to Camberwell
1811	Authority for Royal Arsenal Canal
	St Nicholas Bay Harbour and Canterbury Canal Act
1812	Regent's Canal Act
	Sussex Ouse Navigation opened to Upper Ryelands Bridge
	Weald of Kent Canal Act
	Royal Clarence Ship Canal proposed
1813	Wey and Arun Canal Act
1816	Wey and Arun Canal opened
1817	Royal Arsenal Canal completed
	Act for Portsmouth & Arundel, Chichester, and Portsea Canals
1820	Regent's Canal opened
1822	Chichester Canal opened
	Portsea Canal opened
1823	Work commenced on Grosvenor Canal
	Portsmouth & Arundel Canal completed
1824	Kensington Canal Act
	Hertford Union Canal Act
	Thames and Medway Canal opened
1825	Baybridge Canal Act
	Canterbury Navigation and Sandwich Harbour Act
	Grosvenor Canal opened
1826	Grand Surrey Canal, Peckham Branch opened
1828	Kensington Canal opened
1829	Isle of Dogs Canal closed
1830	Hertford Union Canal opened
	Portsea Canal disused

There had been an attempt to promote a canal to Basingstoke in 1770 and a bill was presented to Parliament. However, it was lost due to improvements that were being carried out on the Thames at that time. Although the Act for the Basingstoke Canal was passed in 1778 no work was done while the war with America continued or during the severe recession that followed, and it was not until 1788 that William Jessop was appointed surveyor and consultant engineer, and the Pinkerton Brothers engaged as contractors for the work. Construction began from the River Wey at Woodham via Woking, Brookwood, Frimley, Ash, Dogmersfield, Odiham and Greywell Tunnel to Basing and Basingstoke; the canal was opened to Basingstoke in September 1794. The canal was 37½ miles long, with twenty-nine locks taking barges 82ft 6in by 14ft 6in carrying 50 tons. The tunnel at Greywell was 1,200yd long, the twenty-fourth longest tunnel in Britain. The canal was a financial disaster. It had cost £153,462, picked up far less trade than expected and never paid a dividend. The canal's existence was seriously threatened by the London and Southampton Railway during the 1830s and the canal company finally went into liquidation in 1866.

The canal's history from then on was one of new companies and their liquidation, with a consequential effect upon the navigation's maintenance and trade. This can be summarised as follows:

1866	Basingstoke Canal Navigation Company goes into liquidation
1866-1874	Canal in hands of receiver
1874-1878	William St Aubyn — Surrey & Hants Canal Company
1878-1880	Canal in hands of receiver
1880	Messrs Dixon and Ward
1880	J. B. Smith
1880-1882	Surrey and Hampshire Canal Corporation Ltd
1882-1883	Canal in hands of receiver
1883-1887	London and Hampshire Canal and Water Co Ltd
1887-1895	Canal in hands of receiver
1895-1896	Sir Frederick Hunt
1896-1900	Woking, Aldershot and Basingstoke Canal and Navigation Company
1900-1905	Canal in hands of receiver
1905	William Carter
1905-1908	Joint Stock and Finance Corporation
1908-1909	London and South Western Canal Company
1909-1914	William Carter
1914-1919	Basingstoke Canal Syndicate Ltd
1919-1923	William Carter
1923-1937	A. J. Harmsworth
1937-1949	Weybridge, Woking and Aldershot Canal Co
1949-1973/5	New Basingstoke Canal Co
1973/5 onwards	Surrey and Hampshire County Councils

In 1901 when the brickworks at Up Nately closed, the regular coal trade from Basingstoke ceased. The last boat to reach Basingstoke arrived in February 1914 after a three-month journey. Despite this downward trend, a degree of restorative work was carried out during the period 1912-14, which enabled a considerable trade to be done during World War I.

With the end of the war, trade began to dry up and in 1920 regular trade above Woking ceased. In 1932, Greywell Tunnel collapsed and much of the land above that point was sold off. From that time, the canal continued to deteriorate and by the 1960s was more-or-less derelict. In 1966 the Surrey and Hampshire Canal Society was formed to campaign for the restoration of the canal. This campaign led to the canal being purchased by the County Councils for the areas through which it ran: Hampshire County Council taking over its section in 1973, and Surrey following in 1975. The canal is currently undergoing restoration throughout, aided by labour under the National Job Creation Scheme. The target set for completion is 1981.

The River Arun had been improved during the sixteenth century as far as Pallingham Quay, with flash locks. In 1785 an Act of Parliament was obtained to make the river navigable to Newbridge by craft of up to 30 tons. In fact two separate canals were made; firstly, a 4½-mile canal from Pallingham to Newbridge with three locks (including one double lock) and an aqueduct; and secondly, Coldwaltham Cut, a 2-mile canal with another three locks and a 375yd tunnel under Hardham Hill which avoided 5 miles of shallow and circuitous river past Pulborough and Greatham. The canal to Newbridge was opened in 1787 and Coldwaltham Cut, three years later. Trade was good until the railways came in the 1850s, but the navigation nevertheless continued. However, the threatened closure of the Wey and Arun Canal sounded the navigation's death knoll. In 1888 the last barge ran from Houghton to Newbridge loaded with chalk and early in 1889 the last barge passed through Hardham Tunnel.

The completion of the Arun navigation in 1790 induced the Earl of Egremont, whose seat was at Petworth, to revive attempts to make the River Rother navigable. In 1791 he obtained an Act to make the river navigable at his own expense, from the Arun at Stopham 11¼ miles to Midhurst with eight locks and a branch from above Stopham Lock 1¼ miles to Haslingbourne Bridge near Petworth, through two more locks. This branch was known as the Petworth Canal and was opened to traffic in 1793. The main line of the Rother Navigation to its termination in Midhurst followed a year later in 1794. The Rother was a success, and trade to Midhurst good. However, in 1861 the railway came to Midhurst and caused a rapid decline in trade. The last barge left the Rother in March 1888; after then the locks fell derelict.

We have already seen that an Act of Parliament in 1665 had authorised the improvement of several rivers in the Hampshire Basin. This Act had provided for the improvement of the Rivers Anton and Test from Andover to Southampton Water, but nothing had come of it. A revival had occured in the 1770s when Robert Whitworth surveyed a line for an Andover Canal to run down the river valleys to Southampton. However, again nothing happened, until another revival in 1788, which eventually led to an Act of Parliament which was passed on 13 July 1789. The canal was 22 miles long with twenty-four locks and finally entered the Test at Redbridge. It was open from Redbridge to Clatford, 2 miles from Andover in January 1794 and reached the town sometime in May.

In 1768, James Brindley had surveyed the line for a canal from Salisbury to Redbridge on the River Test, but the scheme was dropped, to be revived with the Andover Canal in the 1770s, and later again dropped with that scheme. In 1789, with the Andover Canal Bill finally going through Parliament, discussions again took place, but the Salisbury and Southampton Canal Act was not passed until 1795. Work proceeded, with Joseph Hill as resident engineer and Thomas Jenkins as the contractor. Unfortunately, neither proved reliable and Rennie was called in twice to report on the state of the works. In April 1802 the Salisbury section of the canal was navigable from the Andover Canal to West Dean and by January 1803, to the summit level at Alderbury Common. Meanwhile work progressed on the Southampton section of the canal, and with South Marlands Tunnel (under Southampton City Centre) still not completed, the section from Andover Canal at Redbridge to the west entrance to the tunnel, was opened in December 1802. Work appears to have ceased during 1804 with the 880yd canal tunnel still incomplete by some 90yd. Some tolls were still collected during 1804, but by 1810, the canal was in a state of decay. Meanwhile, the Andover Canal was successful in so far as there was considerable local traffic, but not enough for the company to ever pay a dividend. In 1847 the London and South Western Railway obtained authority to purchase the canal when they were constructing their railway from Basingstoke to Salisbury via Andover. In 1849, work on the railway stopped and the canal company took the canal back and purchased the sixteen 18-ton barges currently at work. When the railway was completed to Andover in 1854, railway competition started in earnest and tolls were cut in an effort to retain trade. Eventually, the canal company developed plans to convert their canal into a railway, but eventually when the canal was closed in September 1859, it was the Andover and Redbridge Railway who had purchased the canal in order to effect the conversion.

The last eighteenth-century Sussex waterway was the River Ouse. It appears that the Ouse had been navigable for small craft for some years, for in 1724 it is recorded that small boats used a tributary stream to the powder mills and forge at Marsfield above Shortbridge, and there seems to have been a flash lock where the stream joined the Ouse. In 1788, William Jessop was commissioned to survey the river above Lewes. As a result of his report, an Act of Parliament was passed in 1790 to make the Ouse navigable from Lewes, by Barcombe Mill, Isfield, Fletching and Lindfield '... to Hammer Bridge in the parish of Cuckfield, and to the Extent of the said parish of Cuckfield, and also a Branch of the said river, to Shortbridge, in the parish of Fletching ....' The contract for the work was let to the Pinkertons, who were at that time also working with Jessop on the Basingstoke Canal. By April 1793, the river was navigable as far upstream as Sheffield Bridge, but the money had run out and the navigation was put in the hands of the Receiver while the company set about raising funds. 1805 saw another $1\frac{1}{2}$ miles and two locks completed taking the navigation as far as Freshfield Bridge. In 1806 the company obtained a further Act of Parliament, which enabled them to raise a further £30,000, repealed the section of the 1790 Act which required them to continue the navigation from Hammer Bridge to the far side of Cuckfield Parish, and gave various landowners the right to use surplus water at Isfield Lock and Barcombe Mill. Work commenced, and the navigation reached Lindfield Mill in 1809 and finally Upper Ryelands Bridge in 1812. It is possible that some work was done on the section from there to Hammer Bridge, but it is difficult to trace with any certainty. The navigation from Upper Ryelands Bridge was $22\frac{1}{2}$ miles long with nineteen locks, and the $\frac{3}{4}$-mile branch to Shortbridge. The locks were built 52ft 6in by 13ft 6in to take barges carrying up to 18 tons. Like most of the Sussex rivers, the Ouse was an agricultural waterway, with an upstream traffic of bulk goods such as chalk, coal and stone, and a return traffic of agricultural produce. The Ouse was very much concerned with local trade, and continued quite successfully in this way until yet again railways came to the area, this time in the form of the London and Brighton Railway and later in the mid 1840s, its south coast section from Brighton to Lewes and Hastings. There then followed a succession of toll reductions between 1844 and 1859. In 1858, the railway between Lewes and Uckfield was opened, and it was this more than anything else that finished the navigation. The section above Lindfield became disused in 1861, and the rest of the navigation followed by the end of the decade.

The navigations that we have looked at so far have principally been concerned with local trade and the development of the area surrounding the navigation itself. During the mid-eighteenth century, the importance of London as a centre for national and international trade was growing as the industrial revolution gathered momentum, and exports from the manufacturing industries of the Midlands increased. In 1790, the Oxford Canal had been completed, opening up a water link of sorts via the Thames and while the advantages of this over road transport were outstand-

ing, the unreliable state of the river to Oxford made the journey both lengthy and hazardous. Schemes to improve the water communications from London to the north took two forms. Those utilising the Oxford Canal crystalised into the Hampton Gay project via Aylesbury, Wendover and Uxbridge to Marylebone, capable of taking 60-ton craft, and those which took a more northerly route, from the Thames at Brentford, via Watford, Berkhampstead, Leighton Buzzard, Wolverton, Blisworth, Weedon, and Long Buckley to Braunston. This second line was the successful one, and was to become the Grand Junction Canal.

In July 1792, the promoters appointed William Praed as chairman and commissioned James Barnes as engineer to survey their line. The scheme was prepared for submission to Parliament, and the Grand Junction Canal Act received the Royal Assent in May 1793. The company held their first General Assembly at the Crown and Anchor Tavern in the Strand on 1 June, and formally appointed James Barnes as their engineer '... to devote his whole time to the undertaking and to consider himself as responsible for the works and people employed, and that he be empowered to make contracts for Bricks, Timber and every necessary article; such contracts being laid before the district or General Committee for their approbation, and that he be paid for his services at the rate of Two Guineas per day, and half a guinea per day for his expenses.' Jessop was to act as a consultant and was asked for plans and sections of locks, bridges and tunnels. Barnes proceeded to set out the line and the committee started purchasing land. By December 1793 over 3,000 men were employed on the canal and building proceeded well. During the early months of 1794, the use of the tidal Thames for the company's route to the City was considered unsatisfactory, so on 22 May the committee resolved that they would build an extension from Bull Bridge, Southall to Paddington. The committee quickly set about purchasing land along the Paddington Arm, while work on the Main Line continued. By 5 May 1795, the canal from Brentford to Uxbridge was nearly completed, but complaints were received about the way the work was being done. The committee were forced to issue instructions that:

Mr. Jones and the superintendents... take care when any works are begun that the same be completed as far as possible, and not suffer men to shift about from place to place, and that the canal and lock between Brentford Bridge and the Thames be finished as soon as may be.

The quality of work improved, but the company's concern over finances became acute, as the vast cost and difficulties involved in Blisworth Tunnel, became apparent. Economies were made, and work on branch canals was stopped to concentrate on pushing the main line through to completion. The exception to this was the sum of £5,000 which was reserved for the deep cutting and embankment on the Paddington Arm near the River Brent, and James Barnes was ordered to finish setting out the line to Paddington.

On 21 June 1796 the main line was opened to Weedon, and a boat navigated from Braunston to Weedon for the first time. Meanwhile, work on the arm to Paddington was delayed for long periods of time due to difficult negotiations over the purchase of land, so that it was not until April 1800 that Jessop was able to report that:

> The want of time and bad weather prevented my seeing the line of the Paddington Canal from the point of Junction to the Brent Valley; from hence to Paddington everything is in forwardness except the embankment over the Brent and the deep cutting thro' the hill to the south of it, if about 220 men can be kept on those parts of the works I can see nothing to prevent the canal from being open to Paddington at Christmas.

The Paddington Arm was eventually opened on 10 July 1801, which meant that the waterway route from London to the North via the Oxford and Coventry Canals was open, apart from Blisworth Tunnel, which was by-passed by a tramway until its completion in March 1805.

Meanwhile, in London, the Isle of Dogs Canal had first been proposed to the Court of Common Council of the City of London in 1796, although it was not until 1798 that the firm of Dance, Jessop and Walker were commissioned to survey the line of the canal. They reported that:

> This canal is proposed to be dug to the depth of six feet below the mean level of the water, its width at bottom to be seventy-two feet and at the water's surface at Common Spring Tides, One Hundred and Seventy Six Feet. Each Entrance of this canal is to be provided with two pair of gates, one pair pointing upwards and the other downwards so that without having a current through the canal vessels may be admitted either way and pass through with convenience and safety.

The Isle of Dogs Canal Act passed through Parliament in 1799. Twice, the promoters ran out of money, and applied to Parliament for more, but despite these problems, by July 1805, the canal was:

> ... nearly finished, and was to have been opened with great pomp on the 12th August, when, about twelve o'clock, being near high tide, while a number of people were at work at the extremity next the river, they were suddenly alarmed by a hissing noise, and the appearance of water entering from below. Scarcely had they time to make a precipitate retreat when the outward dam burst with astonishing violence; and what a minute before was dry land was instantly covered with twelve feet of water: the second dam, about fifty yards further on, composed of logs of wood twelve inches thick, besides a strong diagonal log by way of a bar, was in like manner forced by the current, and this amazing strong bar snapped in two, as if it had been a piece of lath. The canal was immediately filled as far as the second flood-gate next to Limehouse, which being shut happily resisted the force of the current.

Finally, the canal was opened on 9 December 1805. It had a fairly uneventful history from then on, other than a permanent shortage of finance, and was finally purchased by the West India Dock Company and converted into a dock in 1829.

Of the few London born canal engineers, perhaps the most well known, most unlucky and unsuccessful, was Ralph Dodd. His schemes were prolific, but those completed under his direction, very few. In London, he proposed three waterways: in 1799 the Thames and Medway Canal and in 1800 both the Grand Surrey Canal and Croydon Canal. The Thames and Medway Canal was to join the Thames at Gravesend, to the Medway at Strood. He proposed a canal 9 miles long on the level, 48ft wide and 7ft deep with river locks and basins at either end. At first, no tunnels were proposed although the cutting through the escarpment between the two rivers was estimated to be 84ft deep at its deepest point.

During 1800, the Act passed through Parliament and Dodd began cutting the canal. By the end of 1801, the four miles from Gravesend to Higham had been cut, as had the basin at Gravesend. By this time, money was running a little short, so Ralph Walker was called in to advise the shareholders. Walker proposed a line somewhat to the west of Dodd's which shortened the canal by $\frac{3}{8}$ mile but increased the depth of cuttings to 100ft. Another Act of Parliament authorised the deviation but little appears to have been done until 1808, when Walker was again called in, but this time he recommended a line even further to the west from Higham Street direct to a point nearer Rochester Bridge, with a long tunnel instead of a deep cutting. This required a further Act of Parliament, which was passed in 1810. Before the tunnel was started, a further Act of 1818 authorised the raising of a further £100,000. The tunnel was started in April 1819 and finally completed on 6 May 1824. The canal was opened on 14 October.

At 4012yd, Higham Tunnel was the second longest canal tunnel built in Britain, being exceeded in length only by Stanedge Tunnel on the Huddersfield Narrow Canal, which is 5,415yd. Higham, however, was a wide tunnel being from $26\frac{1}{2}$ft to 30ft wide with a tow path, whereas Stanedge was a mere 7ft 1in, with no towpath.

The majority of craft using the canal were sailing barges which were unable to pass in the tunnel, and as trade picked up the congestion forced the company to close the canal for ten weeks during early 1830 in order to build a passing place. The tunnel was opened out for about 200ft at the point where the valley above was nearest to the tunnel arch, producing a 100ft-deep rock sided cutting with a small basin.

Despite a steady trade, the canal was never a financial success, and during the early 1840s, the company considered various schemes to convert the canal to a railway, before finally deciding to go ahead and effect a conversion themselves in February 1844. A single track railway was built alongside the canal as far as Higham and then through the tunnel, with one rail on the towing path and the other supported on timbers above the canal. The Thames and Medway Canal and the Gravesend and Rochester Railway continued in co-existence for 18 months, when the canal and railway were sold to the South-Eastern Railway, who filled in the canal from Higham to Frindsbury, opening their double track line through the tunnel on 23 August 1847.

In 1799 Ralph Dodd was also commissioned by various members of the gentry of Kent and Surrey, to survey a canal from Croydon to the Thames. Dodd visited the area and reported back:

Exploring the country for the desirable improvement of a navigation from Croydon to the Thames, I found the most advisable line would be to take a departure from the town of Croydon, at Parson's Mead or Meadow, thence to pass north, nearly parallel to the London Road, which it crosses, a little above Broad Green; then running nearly east, inclining to the north, across the common to Woodside; then inclining considerably more to the north down the valley at the west of Beckenham, continuing the same route close under Sydenham; thence to Perry Street, leaving both these places on the west, and Southend on the east; from thence passing down near the back of the town of Lewisham, leaving that on the east from where the line gradually curves to the west of north; passing to the west of Deptford, it runs nearly in a straight line to a little below the King's Mill at Rotherhithe, and then unites with the Thames: I conceive this is the properest place to join that great river of commerce. Since the chief part of the presumed tonnage up this canal will be coals, it will therefore immediately open into that part of the Pool most frequented by colliers, whence the canal barges might immediately receive from the ship, and pass the freight to any part of the canal, without reloading or reshipping them into other craft. ... I am happy to observe, in the proposed line there would be no expensive tunnel, aqueducts, or numerous bridges. ... Taking into consideration all the concurrent circumstances which would attend a canal navigation in this county, I recommend this navigation to be upon a small scale, with inclined planes instead of locks, and in many places paved fords instead of bridges. The canal not to exceed 3 feet and $\frac{1}{2}$ depth within soil, 24 feet at top, with proportionable slopes to the bottom. ... Boats from 10 to 20 tons may be navi-

gated upon this canal; but probably those of 10 tons would be found most convenient, as one horse can draw 6 or 8 in a fleet linked together, which would be found extremely convenient as one or more of them may be left at the place her loading is consigned to, without detaining a large and inconvenient barge to land a small portion of her cargo.

The promoters did nothing for some time, and then asked John Rennie for his proposals. In October 1800, Rennie reported with two alternative schemes, on a line through Penge Common, Sydenham, Brockley, New Cross and Deptford to the Thames at Rotherhithe. His first scheme was for a canal with inclined planes, taking 5-7 ton boats, costing about £46,516. The second was for a locked canal, taking 20-25 ton craft of up to 75ft × 7ft and costing about £64,100. The scheme with inclined planes was favoured, and a Bill was presented to Parliament.

In the meanwhile on 14 November 1800, Dodd had presented his third set of proposals to a general meeting of prospective shareholders in the Grand Surrey Canal, at the London Tavern. There is no doubt of the welcome he received:

It is the opinion of this meeting that the execution of a navigable canal as surveyed and laid down by Mr. Dodd and passing from the Thames at Rotherhithe to Deptford, Peckham, Camberwell, Walworth, Newington, Kennington, Vauxhall, Stockwell, Clapham, Streatham, Balham Hill, Upper and Lower Tooting, Mitcham, Croydon, Merton, Morden, Kingston, Malden, Ewell and Epsom with collateral cuts to various towns in its vicinity (which canal may in time be extended by way of Southampton to Portsmouth) will be forming a cheap, certain and easy water conveyance for all kinds of articles be productive of the most important advantages to the particular parts through which the canal passes to the metropolis and to the nation in general and also afford to Government an opportunity to execute collateral cuts into His Majesty's Dockyard and Victualling Office at Deptford.

In April 1801 the Surrey and Kent Canal Bill reached the House of Lords, where it was slightly amended. Unfortunately, it was thrown out by the Commons, so a fresh bill was introduced, leading to the Grand Surrey Canal Act being passed on 21 May 1801. With the passing of the Grand Surrey Act, the Croydon Canal Shareholders altered their line slightly to join the Grand Surrey Canal two miles from its junction from the Thames.

One of the major advantages of inclined planes was their saving of water, but shortly after the Croydon Canal Act was passed, it was decided that reservoirs could be built to hold sufficient water to supply the canal without pumping. The inclined planes were forthwith dropped in favour of a locked canal, and construction proceeded. In April 1808 the company applied to Parliament for powers to raise more money; by early 1809 the canal had reached Norwood, and on 22 October was opened for traffic to the canal basin in Croydon:

> The proprietors met at Sydenham and there embarked on one of the Company's barges which was handsomely decorated with flags. At the moment of the barge moving forward an excellent band played 'God Save the King' and a salute of 21 guns was fired.

In his *Cyclopaedia*, Rees wrote of the canal:

> From the Grand Surrey Canal (level with an ordinary high tide in the Thames) to the top of Plowgarlic hill, 1¼ mile, is a rise of 70 feet, by 12 locks; thence for ½ a mile it is level, and thence for ¾ of a mile to the beginning of Forest wood, there is a rise of 79½ feet, by 13 single and one double locks; from there to Croydon, 7 miles, it is level. The locks upon this canal are 60 feet long and 9 feet wide; each lock has a groove for stop-planks at its head, but no paddle-weirs; the waste water is intended to run over the upper gates. This company are to have a bason for their boats to lie in at Rotherhithe, on the southeast side of the Grand Surrey entrance bason, and another by the high road near Croydon town. There are seven road bridges and 30 accommodation swing-bridges. On the top and northern slope of Plowgarlic hill, there is a considerable deep-cutting and others in Sydenham and on Penge common; and near Selhurst wood is a considerable embankment. On Sydenham common there is a reservoir of 10 or 15 acres supplied in wet times by a feeder out of an adjoining vale, and into which its waste or over fall is to be when full; there is another reservoir on Norwood common, which, with the long summit-pound on so tenacious a soil, will be sufficient, it is presumed to supply the locks....

While the Croydon Canal was being constructed, the Grand Surrey Canal Company had pursued the first phase of their line, from Rotherhithe and Deptford, to Camberwell and Walworth to Kennington and the collateral cuts to Peckham and Borough. They advertised in the press, advising landowners to make good their title ready for purchase. Land negotiations were lengthy and complicated, and it was not until February 1802 that the committee advertised for tenders to excavate the canal.

Over the next year or so, as a result of proposals made by John Hall, the shipowner, the plans for a small basin by the Thames changed to a more elaborate dock, thus changing the emphasis of the Company's operation. Construction efforts were channelled towards the dock, but even then problems arose with a lack of navvies due to both harrassment from the Navy pressgangs and the seasonal demands that hay-making put on the availability of both men and horses. By 1804 the company was beset with financial difficulties, which resulted in cuts in the quality of work as economies were made. April 1805 saw the company almost completely out of money. Rowe, their engineer (Dodd had been dismissed in 1802, since he failed to devote enough time to this particular project) reported that £3,000 would see the canal completed to within ½ mile of the Camberwell Road. Work continued on the dock, and in December 1806 Ralph Walker (who had succeeded Rowe as engineer) was ordered to stake out the line of the Peckham Branch. The company were by this time anxious to see at least a part of their works open for trade, and so made much of the opening of the dock on 13 March 1807. There was much pomp, festivity, music, food and drink.

Throughout 1807, much correspondence passed between the Croydon and Grand Surrey Canal companies, as the former sought reassurance from the latter that the Grand Surrey Canal would be open from the Thames to the Croydon canal, by the time that canal was completed. The reassurance was forthcoming, but the Croydon company complained that the dock was obstructed by timber. The Grand Surrey committee did little to remove this problem permanently, but made arrangements to improve it periodically, such as when threatened by legal action in December 1809.

The Grand Surrey Canal company applied to Parliament for a further Act, in June 1807, to enable them to raise funds to continue their line to Rushey Common. By August, matters had progressed far enough for Walker to survey the collateral cuts to Butt Lane and Peckham, and the main line from Kennington Common to Vauxhall. In October, the committee inspected the line and found odd stretches started between the Kent Road and Camberwell. In June 1808, there was another move to complete the canal to the Camberwell Road, but the Peckham branch had to wait until August 1825 for construction to start and May 1826 before it was completed.

In 1855, the canal company finally gave in to its dock interests, changing its name to the Grand Surrey Docks and Canal Company, and in 1864 merging with the Commercial Docks Company. After World War II the canal was abandoned from Wells Way to Walworth and in 1960 the Walworth end was drained. The Surrey Docks were closed in October 1970, and on 4 March 1971 the last barge locked out of the canal, and the entrance was sealed.

The Croydon Canal Company operated as carriers in their own right, and these activities considerably helped the company's financial situation. Even so, the canal never did more than break even. In 1834, Joseph Gibbs surveyed the line of the canal, to consider its suitability for use as a railway. His report was favourably accepted by the promoters of the London and Croydon Railway, and they attempted to purchase the canal. Negotiations as to price lasted for about two years, until the matter was settled by arbitration at £40,259, plus 1 shilling for non-existent profits. The contract was completed on 21 July 1836, and navigation ceased on 22 August.

At the time when the Croydon Canal was being promoted, another company had been considering a canal from Wandsworth to Croydon, but following a report from William Jessop, they changed their plans. The Act for the Surrey Iron Railway was passed a few weeks prior to that for the Croydon Canal. It allowed for a basin by the Thames at Wandsworth, to act as a transhipment point from river to rail. This basin was in fact a short canal (later known as MacMurray's Canal) which was opened on 9 January 1802: 'The first barge entered the lock amidst a vast number of spectators, who rejoiced at the completion of this part of the important and useful work.'

The canal continued in use long after the Surrey Iron Railway was abandoned in 1846, until it too fell into disuse after World War I and was filled in.

Two canals constructed in Kent in the early 1800s were promoted by the government, and not with navigation as their primary use, but defence. The first of these was the Royal Military Canal. The canal was suggested by Lt Col Brown, Assistant Quartermaster General, Royal Staff Corps of Field Engineers, at a time when invasion by Napoleon was feared, and the War Ministry were considering ways of defending the low-lying land that made up Romney Marsh between Hythe and Winchelsea. In September 1804 Brown surveyed the coast and suggested that since the shore batteries were too far apart to be effective once the enemy had reached the beach, construction of a canal from Shorncliffe, in front of Hythe under Lympne Heights to West Hythe and along the rear of Romney Marsh by Appledore to the River Rother, would contain them. By building the 19-mile canal, which would be on the level throughout, with just one lock where it joined the Rother at Iden, 30 miles of coastline would be covered.

Brown's proposals were forwarded to Sir David Dundas, Commander, Southern District who commented: 'Such a ditch or Canal would not be totally unproductive and be of use for Commercial or Husbandry purposes. Floating Defense would be moveable and manageable, and contribute much to its strength and the quick movement of troops.'

The canal scheme passed up through the machinery of bureaucracy to be authorised by Pitt within two weeks of its conception. By the end of October 1804 there was talk of extending the canal from the Rother at Rye, to Cliff End. John Rennie was retained as consultant engineer, and construction started, using contractors. In his report on the undertaking, Rennie recommended that the canal be joined to the Rother with a navigation lock capable of admitting craft from Rye Harbour. He went on to say that should this junction be above Scots Float Sluice, then that sluice must also be rendered passable for craft. Unfortunate-

ly, the contractors fell behind in their work, and it was finished under the direction of the Quartermaster General of the Forces.

Despite these, and other problems, the canal was completed from Shorncliffe to the Rother in July 1806. Work on Iden Lock was not started until October 1807, and took nearly a year to complete; the lock being opened to navigation in September 1808, following great difficulties with its foundations. The lock was equipped with three sets of gates, a conventional pair of mitre gates at the 'top' or canal end, and two pairs at the river end, one pointing in either direction. The extra pair were intended to keep out the river in times of flood or spring tides.

The canal was used for carrying goods immediately, both by the Military, and in 1810 with the opening of the canal to the public, by a regular packet boat service started between Hythe and Iden Lock. Unfortunately this only lasted for three summers. In 1812 canal tolls at £576 reached their peak, although the trade on the canal remained fairly constant into the 1860s. Trade then rapidly fell off, but surprisingly, the last barge did not pass through Iden Lock until December 1909. The lock fell into disrepair in 1910. A couple of years later, P. Bonthron wrote of the canal, in his *My Holidays on Inland Waterways*:

> The canal serves no commercial purpose whatever, and might be said to start as it were from nowhere in particular, and along the whole course there are no business places of any description. It is from 30 to 40 feet wide with about four feet depth of water.... There is little obstruction on the canal and only one lock, at the Rye end, which leads to the sea, but this is not now in use.... considering it is a disused canal, it is kept in excellent order.

The other government-promoted waterway was the Royal Arsenal Canal at Woolwich. The canal was the brainchild of Lt Col Pilkington, Commanding Royal Engineer at Woolwich. During 1810 he conceived of the canal as a method of preventing unauthorised personnel crossing the eastern boundary of the arsenal. As an afterthought, he incorporated a depth of 10ft in his proposals, in order that it should be deep enough to admit cargo vessels to timber wharves that he proposed to build within the arsenal. In July 1810 he wrote to Lt Gen Morse, Inspector General of Fortifications, outlining his plan and estimating that it would cost £1,338 6s 8d for a 45ft-wide canal. Due to military bureaucracy, it was not until May 1811 that Pilkington received authority to proceed and obtain permission to construct the canal from the Commissioners of Sewers. Following this, tenders were sought for the work, so that it was another year before cutting the canal started. By 1814, William Bough, the contractor, had nearly completed the main line of the canal, but ancillary works continued for some years until the waterway was completed in 1817. It had cost a total of

£15,000: £2,500 for the main line and branch, and £12,500 for the lock and wing walls. Initial opinion as to the utility of the canal was enthusiastic, but declined after the first few years. Some money was spent between 1850 and 1852 when mud was cleared away to encourage use of the canal by coasting vessels, but little came of this. The upper part of the canal was filled in over the period between 1926 and 1936 at a cost of £15,420, and the remainder was obliterated with the closing of the arsenal and the development of Thamesmead in the mid-1970s.

The development of the Grand Junction Canal in the light of its bringing long distance trade to London for the first time has already been mentioned. The impact of the opening of the Paddington Arm upon the company's revenue had been incredible; the impact of the completion of the main line, upon the opening of Blisworth Tunnel, was unbelievable. It is perhaps understandable that schemes should be put forward to bring the canal further into the heart of the City and extend it towards the docks. There had been schemes for a North London Canal during the 1770s, and petitions were presented to Parliament but nothing came of them.

Once again, it was the ill-fated engineer Ralph Dodd, who, in 1802 proposed a canal from the Thames near Bell Wharf, to the Whitechapel Road, Hackney, Dalston, Clapton, Tottenham, Edmonton and Enfield to join the Lee at Waltham Abbey. Unfortunately, this particular scheme of Dodd's came to nothing, as did a concurrent project for a 7-mile waterway from the London Docks at Wapping, via the Whitechapel Road, Kingsland Road, and Edgware Road to join the Grand Junction Canal at Paddington. The City had to wait until 1810, when Thomas Homer approached the Grand Junction Canal Committee, with a vague plan for a canal from their basin at Paddington to the Limehouse Cut. Homer then met John Nash, who was at the time laying out Marylebone Park for the Commissioners of Woods and Forests. Nash was enthusiastic, seeing the canal's scenic value and thinking that it may enhance his works. Nash joined the provisional committee and obtained permission from the Prince Regent for the canal to be named after him. The scheme crystallised into an 8-mile canal with twelve locks, and tunnels at Islington and the Edgware Road. In August 1811 a prospectus was issued extolling the new canal's virtues and estimating its cost to be £280,000:

> Considering but for a moment the vast trade carrying on, and the numerous Manufactures in the very populous parts of London, upon the North of the River Thames, extending for several miles, and even far North of the line of the intended Canal, the Mind must be at once impressed with an Immensity of Traffic that must necessarily be carried upon it when executed, but cannot possibly contemplate the Magnitude and Extent of it.

The promoters presented their bill to Parliament, and after a somewhat stormy passage, the Act was finally passed, and the proprietors held their first meeting on 10 August 1812 at the Freemason's Tavern in St Giles-in-the-Fields. James Morgan was appointed engineer and was immediately ordered to stake out the line of the canal. Thomas Homer was appointed superintendent. Various plans were produced for the canal's route through the Marylebone Park, and eventually the fifth version was agreed, with Nash's help. Tenders were invited for excavating the canal from Paddington as far as the Park, and that of James Tate was accepted. While construction of the initial stages of the canal proceeded, the committee concerned themselves with plans for engineering works such as tunnels and locks, and negotiations for the purchase of land. Land negotiations became very involved, with certain discussions (such as that with a Mr Agar) taking years to conclude. Construction of the canal was not without incident, for instance that in September 1813:

> A shocking accident occurred on Friday week at the Regent's Canal, close to Chalk Farm. A few minutes before eleven o'clock, as the workmen were preparing to fill some waggons, twelve men who were lately taken, not being aware of the danger, ventured too close in undermining the bank, at a depth of 25 feet when suddenly the bank fell in, and completely buried them; eight of them were dug out alive, but four with their legs and arms broke, and the other four much bruised; six of the eight are in such a state that their recovery is not expected. After a length of time four more were dug up quite dead, and their bodies removed to the canteen for the Coroner's Inquest.

By 1 June 1814 the canal from Paddington to the Hampstead Road was complete except for a few yards at Maida Hill Tunnel; the collateral cut at Regents Park was underway, and preparations had been made at Islington Tunnel. Initially the excavation of the tunnel at Islington went well, as James Morgan reported on 28 January 1815: '... Four pits have been sunk; 140 yards of the tunnel are completed; and 368 yards of Heading have been driven....' And two months later 250 yards of tunnel had been completed, together with 500 yards of heading: '... there is now a communication between the four shafts, which are at work and the range is a very good one; the two remaining shafts are about to be immediately sunk....'

In fact Islington Tunnel proved to be more difficult to construct than had first been thought, especially as the committee had expressed the opinion that '... when the extensively fated consequences of a failure in the tunnel at any future time, both to lives and properties, are considered, your committee are quite of opinion that considerations of economy ought to be made subordinate to those of providing the

16

utmost security against such a catastrophe.'

Construction continued, and on 12 August 1816 the canal was finally opened from Paddington to the Hampstead Road. Negotiations for land continued, Mr Agar still proving something of a problem, and the company's financial worries became steadily worse. The canal was only completed with help from the government, in the form of a loan or series of loans from the Commission for the Issue of Exchequer Bills, under a scheme to provide work for the unemployed poor. In June 1820 the canal was open from Paddington to the City Road Basin, and finally on 1 August the Regent's Canal was opened throughout.

Yesterday this canal was opened in form by the Earl of Macclesfield, the Chairman, the Deputy Chairman, Colonel Drinkwater, and the Members of the Committee, in the presence of a very numerous and genteel assemblage of persons, who crowded both banks of the Canal throughout the whole line of the procession. The barges and boats, seven in number were profusely ornamented with streamers, and accompanied by two military bands, whose martial and enlivening airs served, not in a little degree to augment the pleasure and interest of the scene. At 11 o'clock, the line of boats entered the tunnel which commences near Battlebridge, and is continued in a direct line near three quarters of a mile thought part of Islington, and emerging at the distance of about 40 feet east of the New River. In something less than half-an-hour, salutes from each shore announced their exit from this subterraneous passage; at this moment the bands struck up the national anthem of 'God Save the King', which was answered with the utmost enthusiasm and fervour by the huzzas of at least 10,000 persons. It having been known that this canal was to be opened on the 1st of August, three barges with manufactured goods, arrived at the wharf in the City Road, from Manchester, immediately as the procession passed. At the Basin at Limehouse, ships of 300 tons can load and discharge with perfect safety and convenience. At six o'clock, the barge containing the Members of the Committee and their friends entered the river, directing their course towards the Custom House stairs from whence they proceeded to the London Tavern to dine. About half after seven the company sat down to dinner.... Upon the toast of 'Prosperity to the Regent's Canal' being drunk, Mr. C. Monroe (one of the Committee for superintending the construction of the canal) rose and observed, that the great undertaking, upon the accomplishment of which he had then to congratulate the meeting, had commenced not many years since. The object of this undertaking was to unite all the canals and navigable rivers of the country with the river Thames, and that object was happily attained....

Trade on the canal rapidly increased from 72,257 tons during the nine months after the opening in 1820, to 288,692 tons in 1822, and 496,058 tons in 1825. Although long distance and fly (non-stop) traffic was encouraged by the company by far the greatest proportion of their trade came from dock traffic rather than from the interior of the country.

On 18 June 1823, Francis Giles, engineer to Sir George Duckett, approached the committee respecting a plan for making a cut from the Lee Navigation, to communicate with the Regent's Canal near Old Ford Bridge. Four months later Duckett himself met the committee, outlined his plans in greater depth and asserting his intention of introducing a petition to Parliament, promised to forward them a copy of the Bill as soon as it was prepared.

Duckett obtained the Act authorising his Hertford Union Canal early in 1824. Cutting the canal brought with it few difficulties, and it was quietly opened early in 1830. The Regent's Canal Company welcomed Duckett's Cut (as it was sometimes called) and anticipated that it would bring them considerable trade from the River Lee. In May 1830 they even agreed to especially low tonnage rates for craft passing along their canal either to or from the Hertford Union.

Unfortunately, trade on the Hertford Union was not up to the level that Duckett had hoped for, and on 15 December 1830 he approached the Regent's Canal committee and outlined his plan to open his canal to the public toll-free until 31 March 1831 in order to encourage trade. Duckett had water supply problems too, and here also, the Regent's Canal helped out over dry periods for several years. In June 1834 the Hertford Union was offered for sale to the Trustees of the River Lee Navigation, but they showed no interest. Trade on the canal remained at a very low level and throughout the 1830s and 1840s Duckett was forever applying to the Regent's Canal Company for concessions for trade using his canal. Finally, on 22 March 1848 with trade practically non-existent, the canal was stanked off at Old Ford, to prevent it taking water from the Regent's Canal. In May 1851 Sir George Duckett put his canal up for sale, but the Regent's Canal Company declined initially, so that it was not until the autumn of 1857 that the Hertford Union Canal was finally purchased and became a part of the Regent's Canal.

Over the latter half of the nineteenth century the Regent's Canal was subject to a large number of schemes for conversion to a railway and it was taken over in 1883 by a new company — The Regent's Canal, City Docks Railway Company — who had authority for a number of different lines. Still, nothing was done, and the canal continued in the face of railway competition, with its various rail/water transhipment points. In 1892, the company changed its name to the North Metropolitan Railway and Canal Co, and then in 1904, to the Regent's Canal and Dock Company.

Since the 1830s, all waterways on the London-

Birmingham-Manchester route (with one exception) had co-operated in a toll-cutting war to fight railway competition. As years went by they discovered that they had a number of common problems and perhaps it was inevitable that close co-operation at least should come about. In 1914 the Grand Junction Canal and the Regent's Canal companies formed a joint committee of directors, who met once a month. During World War I both canals came under the auspices of the Southern District Sub-Committee of the Canal Control Committee of the Board of Trade. After the war, the two canals continued to work closely together, until on 13 April 1926 Mr W. H. Curtis, Chairman of the Regent's Canal and Dock Company, reported to his committee:

that he had instructed Mr. R. C. Martin, one of the partners of Messrs. Deloitte, Plinder, Griffiths, & Co. to examine the latest Balance Sheets with statements of Account of the Grand Junction Canal Company with a view to the preparation of a scheme for this company to acquire that undertaking, excluding the Paddington Estate.

Deloitte's report was circulated to the directors in May, and on 16 November the companies exchanged auditors' reports. By the end of the month, the two companies had agreed — in principle — on the merger, although the Regent's Canal Company added the stipulation that the Grand Junction Canal had to make arrangements to acquire the Warwick and Birmingham, Warwick and Napton, and Birmingham and Warwick Junction Canals. This was essential, to ensure that the new company should have control of the London-Birmingham throughroute. The two Acts of Parliament, approving the mergers, received the Royal Assent on 3 August 1928, and on 1 January 1929 the Grand Union Canal Company came into being. The Regent's Canal and Dock Company had paid £140,003 15s 0d for the Warwick canals, and £801,442 2s 7d for the Grand Junction Canal. *Lloyd's List* reported that:

The new amalgamation is regarded as the most important development of the movement to organise Britain's canal system in effective competition with the railway and road transport systems.

The Grand Union Canal Company hoped that they would now be in a good position to encourage trade. They intended to do this in two ways, firstly by improving the design of the craft using the canal, and secondly by providing a wide, barge canal throughout the route from London to Birmingham.

In July 1928 the old Regent's Canal and Dock Company had commissioned a pair of boats, the *George* and the *Mary* from the Steel Barrel Company of Uxbridge. These boats, delivered to the Grand Union Canal Company (GUCC) in March 1929, were to become the prototypes of the Royalty class boats.

During the 1920s and '30s, a number of small carrying companies had difficulties in paying tolls, and in August 1930 Associated Canal Carriers owed the GUCC £609 8s 1d in rent and tonnage. Eventually, the GUCC purchased the entire share capital of this company for £750, and henceforth the ACC became the GUCC's carrying subsidiary. A period of expansion of these carrying activities began in 1931, with the order for six pairs of Royalty Class Boats. In March 1932 Associated Canal Carriers changed their name to the Grand Union Canal Carrying Company and continued the expansion progress with orders for another 174 pairs of boats. Meanwhile, the GUCC initiated a £1 million improvement plan in 1931 which included rebuilding the locks on the Warwick Canals, to 14ft beams, widening all necessary bridges, and also instituting a grand dredging programme. Also in 1931, the Leicester and Loughborough Navigations, and the Erewash Canal were purchased for £55,229, thus giving the company a direct route into Derbyshire and to the River Trent. They then proposed to widen the two flights of locks at Watford and Foxton (at a cost of £143,550) in order to provide a 14ft barge route from the Thames to the Trent. The 1930s and '40s were a period when the GUCC fought to secure bulk traffics, competing with both rail and road interests. In particular, there were tough battles to obtain a share of such traffics as iron and steel from the docks to Birmingham. At the same time, they suffered from a shortage of boatmen:

The difficulty is to get the right men . . . either they won't stay — don't take to the life — or they are not good enough for the job. Yet a good barge captain can make £7 or £8 a week according to the amount of cargo he carries. . . . One objection to the life may be that there is no absolute certainty about where a barge will be at certain times. There are no particular hours of work.

If a family can man a pair of barges and share the earnings that is the ideal way. Those who have the tradition of the canals behind them are able to adapt themselves to the new conditions. It is the new men who are difficult to turn into good barge hands and barge captains.

During World War II this particular problem was alleviated to some extent by women volunteering to crew boats as a form of National Service. After the war, the prospects for the GUCC looked rather brighter. Unfortunately, the Transport Act of 1947 brought the Grand Union Canal, along with most other inland waterways under government control. The Grand Union Canal became a part of the South Eastern Division of the Docks and Inland Waterways Executive of the British Transport Commission. The Act came into force on 1 January 1948, and on this date, the Grand Union Canal Carrying Company also passed into government hands. In November 1948 the independent carrying company of Fellows, Morton and Clayton went into voluntary liquidation and sold out to the government, following a £5,000 loss in the first six months of the previous year — the first time in the company's history. The canals remained with the British Transport Commission, until the 1962 Transport Act brought them under the newly formed British Waterways Board on 1 January 1963. British Waterways quickly reduced their carrying activities and decided to disband their fleet of narrow boats. From hundreds of pairs, the fleet was reduced to just ten pairs, a few of which were retained until the early 1970s.

Another waterway route which served the long distance trade to London, was a scheme to link the rivers Wey and Arun and thus provide a water through-route from London to the South coast and Portsmouth. The Wey and Arun Junction Canal was originally thought of during the closing months of 1810, but was put to a meeting in Guildford on 1 June 1811. Resolutions at the meetings in Guildford and Godalming expressed support for the scheme, and a committee was formed to prepare a petition for Parliament. In the forefront again, was Lord Egremont. In October a prospectus was issued setting out the advantage of the 17-mile navigation and estimating that annual traffic was likely to be in the region of 130,000 tons. Within a month, 132 subscribers had put forward the total proposed capital of £90,000, Lord Egremont having subscribed £20,000. During 1812 negotiations with landowners took place, so that the Bill was not introduced to Parliament until February 1813. The Act received the Royal Assent on 1 April. Josias Jessop was retained as consultant, and designed all the aqueducts, bridges and lock-keeper's cottages, while the resident engineer and clerk of works was May Upton. Zachariah Keppel, a builder from Alfold, contracted to do the work, but unfortunately went bankrupt in December 1814 with only one third of the canal completed. May Upton struggled on, beset by heavy rain over the winter of 1814/15 and a belt of sand along the deep cutting on the summit level. The canal was eventually opened in September 1816 amid much celebration — even the navvies being provided with roast oxen and 200 gallons of ale. The canal, as built, from Shalford on the River Wey, to Newbridge on the Arun Navigation, was 18½ miles long, with twenty-three locks and two aqueducts, at Gosden and Drungewick.

Unfortunately, trade fell far short of what had been expected, remaining between 15-20,000 tons per annum for most of the canal's life (a peak of over 23,000 tons was reached in 1839-40), but this was only maintained with a succession of toll reductions in the face of constant railway competition at the northern end. With the opening of the London, Brighton and South Coast Railway in 1865, the canal's death knoll was sounded, and in 1868 an Act of Parliament authorised its closure, although the last loaded boat passed through the canal to Bramley Wharf in June 1872.

In 1815, when the Wey and Arun Canal was nearing completion, a group of promoters who were considering providing a canal from the River Arun to Portsmouth, approached the Admiralty for approval. The Admiralty consulted Rennie, who was in favour of the project and when asked for advice by the promoters, employed Francis and Netlam Giles to conduct a survey. Rennie then recommended a barge canal, 33ft wide and 4ft 6in deep, 12 miles long from the tidal Arun at Ford, to Salterns near Birdham, in Chichester Harbour, with four locks (two at either end) and a 1¼-mile branch from Hunston to Chichester. The route from Salterns was via Thorney Channel, Langstone Channel and Langstone Harbour to enter the Portsea Canal at Milton. The Portsea Canal was 2½ miles long, with two locks at Milton, and ran across Portsea Island, to a basin at Halfway Houses, Portsmouth. There was also to be a 1¼-mile cut across the top of Portsea Island, via Cosham, giving access to Portsmouth Harbour.

The promoters obtained their Portsmouth and Arundel Canal Act in 1817, but the first sod was not cut until 20 August 1818 at Ford. Work also began at Merston on the Chichester section in September, and must have been considered of more importance, as the Ford-Hunston section was opened last. Although the main criteria was the completion of the London-Portsmouth long distance route, the Proprietors had identified the potential in the trade to Chichester itself and the benefits of avoiding unnecessary transhipment of cargoes, and in 1818 applied for a second Act of Parliament, to allow them to build the Salterns-Hunston-Chichester Section as a ship canal, to take 100-ton vessels, and the Portsea Canal to take 150-ton vessels. The extra expense was covered by the decision not to proceed with the cut through Cosham.

Chichester Canal basin was filled with water on 27 December 1821, and the Chichester Canal opened on 9 April 1822. Next came the Portsea Canal on 19 September 1822 and finally the 9¾-mile Ford-Hunston Section was opened on 26 May 1823. The company had two pumping stations, at Milton top lock and at Ford top lock, to provide water to the two summit levels. Unfortunately, they had problems with salt water entering the canal and percolating into local water supplies. The problem at Milton was so serious that in the end the company was forced to drain the Portsea canal. In 1830 the Portsea Canal was formally closed, although of course it had not been used for some time (it had been drained for at least 3 years), and the company opened their new Portsbridge Cut which gave direct access, across the top of Portsea Island, into Portsmouth Harbour. Efforts were made to increase the level of the London-Portsmouth trade, but with little success. However, some bullion was moved from Portsmouth by canal, and for a few years in the early 1830s, the level of general goods improved. However, the Portsmouth and Arundel Canal only continued due to support from the Chichester line, and the company's finances were tottering. As a result of railway competition, the Ford-Hunston section of the canal ceased to be used after 1847. Traffic on the remaining section of the canal, from Salterns Lock to Southgate Basin, Chichester had fallen to about 4,000 tons in the 1880s and in 1888 a group of shareholders applied for an order to wind up the company. The order was granted and following an Act of Parliament in 1892, the Chichester Canal was transferred to Chichester Corporation. Trade gradually dwindled even more, and the last commercial traffic used the canal in 1906. In 1928, the canal was finally abandoned, but the section from Salterns Lock to Manhood End was re-opened in 1932 for yacht moorings. In 1957 the canal was sold to West Sussex County Council for £7,500.

An Act of Parliament of 1807 had authorised the improvement of the tidal River Adur, 14 miles from Shoreham to Bines Bridge, to make it navigable for barges drawing up to 3ft. Work was carried out, and the river was made navigable for barges drawing 4ft, and the trustees collected a toll of ½d or 1d per ton. In 1824, a group of seven promoters, lead by Lord Selsey and Sir Charles Merrick Burrell, commissioned May Upton, previously engineer on the Wey and Arun Canal to survey the Adur from Bines Bridge to Baybridge. Upton reported back for a navigation 3⅜ miles long, with two locks 75ft × 12ft 6in at Partridge Green and West Grinstead giving a rise of 14ft, and a river channel 28ft wide at the top, and 4ft deep. He estimated the cost at £5,957 16s 7d and expected the work to be completed within three years. The promoters applied to Parliament for authority to construct their Baybridge Canal, and the Act received the Royal Assent on 22 June 1825.

The navigation was intended solely for local use, with the main upstream traffic being manure, with return cargoes of local agricultural produce. The authorised tolls were as follows:

Beech, Gravel or other materials in the repair of Roads, Chalk, Dung, Mould, Soil, Compost, or other articles (except Lime) to be used for the manuring of Land	2d per Ton per mile
Goods, Wares, Articles, Commodities or Merchandize	5d per Ton per mile
Fractions of a Ton, and of a mile, shall not be deemed less than a Quarter	
For Wharfage of any Goods remaining less than Seventy-two Hours	9d per Ton

The opening of the Brighton Railway in 1861 seriously competed with the canal, and in February 1875 the proprietors applied to Parliament for an Act to close it.

The Grosvenor family had owned a large part of Chelsea for centuries. In 1727 Sir Richard Grosvenor leased a plot of land by the Thames to the newly formed Chelsea Waterworks Company, so that they could supply Westminster with water. The company had obtained permission to make cuts from the Thames to convey their water northwards, to be stored in reservoirs between Olivers Mount and Hyde Park, but we know that they were also used by sailing barges, and that flood gates were erected at their eastern entrance to the Thames. In the 1780s there is a mention of wharves on these water courses. During the 1790s and 1810s Lord Grosvenor was looking at the development of his estate and in 1811 had formulated a plan for a canal, but could not proceed with it, as the waterworks lease did not revert until 1826. Despite this, in January 1823 Thomas Thatcher had been instructed to lay out the canal, but complained that he could not proceed until he knew the size of vessels that were to use it. On 21 July Thomas Cundy (the Grosvenor Estate's architect and surveyor) signed a contract with John and William Johnson and Alexander Brice, builders, of Holywell Street, for digging the canal and constructing wharves and the lock etc. The entrance lock was to be 103ft 4in long and 19ft wide, while the canal itself was to be 24ft wide at the bottom, with 9ft 6in banks sloping 1 in 2. The entire volume of the canal, basin, and lay-by sand lock was estimated at 261,640 cubic yards, of which 171,257 cubic yards would be new cutting. Work proceeded well in general, although it slowed during the winter of 1823-4. Summer brought better progress, so that on 12 June 1824 Thatcher was able to report:

Excavation of the Lock pit, the lay by, and canal, the building of the lock nearly compleat, one pair of gates are in the lock, and others will soon be ready — there are about nine hundred feet of the wharf walls in each side of the bridge to their height; and a part of the coping is on. The excavation of the large basin is so far compleat that the earth now in the bottom is for the purpose of backing the walls, the pile driving and the foundations will be commenced in the course of the next week, and the materials in the work [are] exceeding in amount of £12,000....

Over the previous winter Thatcher had serious doubts as to whether the canal would be opened on schedule in April 1825, but in fact it was quietly opened on 5 March. It had cost £33,679 8s 10d to build. The Grosvenor Canal settled down to a peaceful existence. It was only ¾ mile long with one lock at the entrance, and ended in a large basin in Pimlico. Traffic remained steady through most of its life despite the persistent silting problems, which were only overcome by annually draining the canal for a couple of weeks. In 1857, the Victoria Station and Pimlico Railway Act authorised:

... stopping up or appropriating of the Grosvenor Basin, and the using of the same or any part thereof for the purposes of the Railways Stations and works [and]... the diverting or narrowing of the Grosvenor Canal and the towing path between or near to the points at which the Grosvenor Canal passes under Ebury Bridge and Eccleston Bridge respectively.

The Earl of Grosvenor (now the Marquis of Westminster) sold the relevant land to the railway for £112,735 and turned his attention to repairs on the remaining section of the canal. In the 1880s and 1890s trade on the canal diminished, so that the closure in 1899 of the upper section between Ebury and Eccleston Bridges passed without comment. The canal was now only 550yd long and used almost exclusively by the City of Westminster for the barging of refuse. Thus it is not surprising that in 1906 the Marquis sold the canal and its surrounding land to the council for £95,000. The canal continued in much the same state for some years, until it was closed between 12 July 1928 and 3 July 1929 while the lock and lower section were rebuilt. At the time of writing the canal is still in use, and is used exclusively by the council, and their agents Cory Lighterage, for barging refuse to the Thames Estuary.

The Kensington Canal was a contemporary of the Grosvenor in many ways. A scheme of 1822 to widen and deepen the creek from Stamford Bridge, Fulham to Counters Bridge, came to nothing but paved the way for 'An Act for Widening, Deepening, Enlarging, and making Navigable a certain Creek called Counter's Creek, from or from near Counter's Bridge, on the Road from London to Hammersmith, to the River Thames....'; promoted in 1824 by Lord Kensington, Sir John Scott Lillie and others. The Act received the Royal Assent on 28 May and by the end of August Mr Stent, the company's clerk had signed a contract with a Mr Hoof, for building the canal, and work had begun. Work proceeded well and John Rennie, the consulting engineer estimated the cost at £34,117 4s 0d and that the canal would be completed within three years. The canal was opened on 12 August 1828 and the company charged a toll of $3\frac{1}{2}$d per ton for manure and 7d per ton for other goods. Things looked good, and there was even a plan to extend the canal northwards $2\frac{1}{2}$ miles through eleven locks to join the Paddington Arm of the Grand Junction Canal. This extension was never built, but the Birmingham, Bristol and Thames Junction Railway, which received Parliamentary authority on 21 June 1836 made the link instead. The BB&TJR purchased the Kensington Canal, from the basin of which their railway was to run, for £10,000 in cash and £26,000 in railway shares. The railway company got down to the business of laying its track, while the Kensington Canal Company began winding up its affairs, to prepare for a speedy takeover. Unfortunately, the railway company seemed in no hurry, so in November 1837, the canal company, still in full possession of its canal, threatened to file a bill in Chancery for specific performance of contract. Finally, the conveyance was signed in August 1839 and the railway company had done a considerable amount of work improving the canal, which was of course their method of achieving a transhipment point with the Thames. Unfortunately, during the end of 1839 and 1840 the canal again deteriorated and complaints rolled in. The major problem was that, of the $1\frac{3}{4}$-mile canal, only the top few hundred yards were non-tidal, so that silting was serious and the canal was only fully navigable for a few hours a day. In 1845, the BB&TJR (now renamed the West London Railway) leased its line to the London & Birmingham Railway and moved to the lockhouse to run its canal. Repairs were put in hand and trade picked up slightly; in fact toll receipts were at their highest so far, but despite this, the directors considered selling the canal, and put negotiations in hand. Eventually, a consortium of companies formed the West London Extension Railway Company, and under their Act of 1859 the canal again changed hands. The canal was quickly handed over, and was filled in from the basin, as far south as Christies Mill, by the Kings Road, to allow for the railway track to be laid. The canal continued with a steady trade, but with silting problems in much the same way as the Grosvenor Canal. In 1947, with the nationalisation of the railways, the canal passed into the hands of the British Transport Commission, and in 1963 to the British Waterways Board. In 1959, the section from the Imperial Gas Works to the Kings Road was abandoned, and in 1967 the motor barge *Rabbie* delivered the last cargo of 23,000 gallons of gas oil from Grays, Essex, to the Imperial Gas Works dock, and more-or-less ended commercial carrying on the Kensington Canal. Today, about 350yd of the canal remain as a tidal creek, alongside Lots Road Power Station.

With the completion of the Kensington Canal in 1828 the main era of navigation building in South-East England drew to a close. By 1830, over 415 miles of canal or river navigation had been constructed with over 297 locks, and that excluding the River Thames. Unfortunately, just as waterway schemes were prolific in the South-East, so too were the railways. Promoters were keen to provide routes for goods and passengers to reach the London Markets and for imports from abroad to leave the docks, and reach the interior of the land. The railways obviously had one great advantage over the waterways and that was speed. Thus those canals and rivers that operated on a small budget were unable to compete, and in many cases were forced to close, while those concerns that were large enough to compete did so by cutting tolls and thus their profitability. Despite this many continued to trade well into the twentieth century, carrying an assortment of bulk cargoes — not least amongst them was of course the great Grand Union Canal.

Only three waterways were constructed during the

period of decline. The first was the Dartford and Crayford Navigation, the second, the Millwall Canal, and the third the ill-fated Romford Canal.

The River Darent from the Thames to Dartford, has been navigable from the earliest times: there were four wharves on the river and seven boats ranging from 3 tons to 15 tons during Queen Elizabeth I's reign. The river was still navigable as a natural stream at the beginning of the nineteenth century. In 1836, there was a scheme for a ship canal to Dartford, but this came to nothing, being lost in Parliament and it was not until May 1939 that the scheme which led up to the Dartford and Crayford Navigation Act came to light. A group of local landowners and businessmen approached the Commissioners of Sewers for the limits extending from Lombards Wall to Gravesend Bridge with a scheme to improve the Dartford and Crayford Creeks, by dredging and making cuts. Unfortunately, the Commissioners were unable — under their terms of reference — to proceed with the scheme, and recommended the promoters to go it alone. James Easton (the engineer who had produced the scheme) and Edward Stoneham (a landowner) held public meetings to put forward their ideas, ending up with the passing of a set of resolutions of approval. They applied to Parliament for authority to do the work, and the Act which was passed on 4 June 1840 set up the Commissioners of the Dartford and Crayford Navigation with a basic charge to improve the creeks and run them as a non-profitmaking concern. In 1841 work commenced on a cut to straighten the navigation from Hibberts Wharf to Great Moorden Reach, but due to a number of problems, including bank slips, it was not opened until 25 March 1844. Traffic on the creeks increased tremendously, so that instead of the expected yearly revenue of about £937 10s 0d, in 1860 they received £1,434 13s 0d. Dredging and deepening continued and in 1879, Edward Easton, the Commissioners' engineer proposed the construction of a lock 200ft by 30ft at the mouth of the creek, which would have the effect of turning the navigation into a dock. He estimated the cost at £40,000, and that it could be repaid out of the normal 3d per ton toll.

Unfortunately, the commissioners rejected the scheme, but as the navigation developed and wharves continued to spring up along its banks, they were forced to reduce the toll to 1d per ton in order to remain non-profitmaking. They discussed the idea of a lock again in December 1892, and in March 1893, recorded that:

The Special Committee appointed at the last meeting reported in reference to the proposition to improve the creek above the Daily Telegraph Paper Mills for the better movement of craft [were] of the opinion that it was desireable to construct a lock in the Dartford Creek near the Telegraph Mills....

Eventually the committee settled on a lock 150ft ×

25ft, costing £3,800 and a further £350 for a lock-keeper's cottage and office. Work proceeded well initially, having been started in the spring of 1894, so that on 13 May 1895, the Commissioners' engineer, Mr W. H. Thomas, was able to report that:

The Lock itself is practically finished, the gates hung, and the machinery for actuating them and the sluices fixed and in working order. The weir is being proceeded with and in about a week will, I expect be sufficiently advanced to necessitate the turning of the traffic through the lock, while the piling is driven across the existing stream and if all goes well three weeks or a month should see the completion of this part of the work.

The lock was open for use on 10 July 1895, but the contractors sent in their account for extras, which raised the contract price for the lock to £4,768 3s 6d and for the Bascule Bridge above the lock to £549 18s 0d.

Traffic in the creeks increased even more than before, and the commissioners employed a superintendent to oversee the creeks and collect tolls. The commissioners continually carried out dredging of the creeks, but in 1906, tolls were once more reduced to 1d per ton as excessive returns were being collected. In 1920, the commissioners considered proposals for modernisation of their lock, but settled for repairs to their current structure. Again in 1927, the matter of creek improvements was raised, and Case and Cunningham, a firm of consulting engineers were commissioned to report upon whether the creeks could be improved by the construction of locks at their mouth, or in any other position nearer the Thames than the present lock; and if such construction was feasible, what would be the estimated cost. They reported on enlarging the present lock; constructing a larger lock at the creek mouth; and, thirdly, constructing a larger lock at, and just above, the junction with Crayford Creek. The third alternative was the recommended one, and the estimated cost was £68,000. Despite favourable reports in the local press, the Commissioners were forced to issue a statement to the effect that they:

... were unable to consider the question of erecting any new locks in the creeks at the present time owing to there being no source from which the money could be raised.

Due to this lack of funds, Case and Cunningham were asked for recommendations to keep the creeks going and they simply recommended dredging above the lock, repairs to the lock and weir and dredging in the lower lock channel. Trade continued as before; dredging continued to be necessary, and in 1954 the lock gates were renewed. The closure of the London Paper Mills in 1968 seriously affected traffic, to the extent of 18,000 tons per annum, and this was followed by a general decline in trade which has continued throughout the 1970s. Trade still continues, but at a lower level than before.

The Millwall Canal Act of 1864 was reminiscent of the old Isle of Dogs Canal. However, the Millwall Canal was intended more to provide wharfage facilities rather than a trans-Isle of Dogs thoroughfare. The canal was absorbed by the Millwall Dock in 1868.

Lastly, we come to the Romford Canal. There had been schemes for a canal to Romford throughout the initial decades of the nineteenth century, in 1809, 1811, 1818, 1820 and 1824. The 1820 scheme even included the use of inclined planes, in place of locks. The idea of a canal to Romford was revived in 1874 by a group of promoters led by Captain G. E. Price, MP, James Gadsden Wainwright, and H. F. Twynam, who engaged the firm of Russ and Minns as engineers to survey the line of the canal. They then applied to Parliament for an Act authorising them to construct the canal, and obtained Royal Assent on 19 July 1875. The Act contained three provisions:

1 A Canal (4 miles, 5 furlongs and 10 yards in length) commencing in the parish of Romford in the County of Essex, near the Romford Station of the Great Eastern Railway, and terminating in the parishes of Dagenham and Hornchurch, or one of those parishes, in the same county, in the River Thames near Havering Great Sluice.

2 A collateral cut or canal about four hundred yards in length wholly in the parish of Dagenham aforesaid.

3 The scouring, dredging, and deepening of the bed, shore and soil of the River Thames at or near any of the works by this Act authorised.

The canal was to have six locks; one by the Thames, a second at Beam Bridge by the New Road (now the A13) and a flight of four locks by the junction with the collateral cut, two miles short of Romford. The estimated cost was £60,000.

Work on the canal started, and by 18 January 1876 lock number two was almost completed, plans for the entrance lock had been approved and the engineers went on to say:

We fully expect that the first section of the canal from the Thames to the Rainham and Barking Road Wharf will be complete and open for traffic by April next; the second section from thence to the locks and Collateral Cut, to the Romford and Rainham Road will also be completed and open by June next, and the whole finished within twelve months from the commencement of the works.

Unfortunately, this was a little optimistic as in March 1876 the company was short of funds and had to apply to Parliament for powers to raise more money. The canal works lay idle. A revival of enthusiasm in 1880 resulted in an extension of Compulsory Purchase Powers, but nothing was done and in 1882 the Romford Canal Company was wound up and the canal was not proceeded with. None of it was ever opened. It was not until 16 October 1912, that the company's land was sold by auction, in Tokenhouse Yard by the Bank of England.

This very brief outline of the history of Inland Navigation in South-East England is the backbone around which life on waterways in the area evolved. The illustrations that make up the bulk of this book portray events which occurred, life as it was, and the scenes as they were, during that evolution. Like the waterways they portray, they are not systematic, but fragmentary, due to the scarcity of photographers during the nineteenth century, the fragility of early negatives and prints, the abilities of the 'archivists' who have stored them, and those of the researcher in locating them. What we have is a fascinating glimpse of the past.

The Thames to the Medway

1

1 Two sailing barges lie, with their sails furled, at Sankey & Co's wharf on Hammersmith Creek, about 1920. The craft on the left is a wooden lighter belonging to Sankey. Hammersmith Creek ran from the Thames, a few hundred yards upstream of Hammersmith Bridge, and on the north bank beyond King Street for up to a mile. Its eastern bank was occupied by wharves, while the western bank was flanked by malthouses which formed a part of the Town Brewery which was founded in 1780 by Joseph Cromwell. The creek was used by barges, up until 1930, and was filled in during 1935 and 1936.

2 Thames sailing barges were constructed with flat bottoms, which not only made them ideal for working in the shallow creeks of the East Coast, but also enabled them to sit quite safely on riverside mud banks at low tide, providing easy access for unloading. By the time that this photograph was taken of *Bluebell* in February 1923 unloading on the mud at Putney, the use of horses and carts (as seen in the *Frontis*) had partially been surpassed by steam lorries.

3 Nash & Miller's barge building yard at Battersea on the tidal Thames, was always a hive of industry, with wooden craft of all types being built. Here, work has stopped while the men pose for the camera. In the foreground are a number of wooden dumb lighters.

2

3

4 Thames sailing barges carried many different cargoes, but perhaps the most spectacular were the hay barges. Known as 'Stackies', they loaded their cargo high up into the rigging and travelled with reefed sails. The hay was carried from the creeks of the Essex coast to the stables of London, and is seen here passing St Paul's Cathedral about 1905.

5 The *John* and the *James* lie empty on the mud at Isleworth Town Wharf. Note the steam launch frozen in the ice, under the trees. The occasion was the 'Arctic' winter of 1891. 'Icebergs' like these could also be seen at the time further down the Thames and in Dartford on the Dartford and Crayford Navigation.

6 Strand-on-the-Green, just downstream of Kew Bridge was the 'home' of a considerable number of sailing barges owned by 'small' operators, and was a popular place for barges waiting for orders or carrying out minor repairs. The sailing barge on the outside of this string has its mast lowered. The three craft in the centre are wooden dumb lighters.

4 St. Paul's Cathedral from the Thames, London

5

6

7 Prior to the construction of a bridge over the Thames at Kew, there had been a ferry nearby known as Powell's Ferry. The proprietor was the father of a Robert Tunstall, and it was he who built the first Kew Bridge. The bridge had eleven arches, of which the central seven were of timber construction. The first stone of this bridge was laid on 29 July 1758 on the Surrey side of the river and was followed by '... an elegant entertainment at the Rose & Crown on Kew Bridge.' The bridge was opened on 4 June 1759, but a few days beforehand the Prince (later to become George III) and Dowager Princess of Wales crossed the bridge, making a present of £200 to the proprietor, and 20 guineas to the workmen. On the opening day, 3000 people crossed the bridge, paying a penny toll.

7

9 A third and final Kew Bridge was built at the turn of the twentieth century and opened in 1903, when a banquet was held in marquees erected on top of the bridge. This third bridge is still in use today.

10 Wooden lighters outside Brentford Gas Works on the Thames in 1926. Those in the background are loaded with coal and await unloading, while those in the foreground are loaded with waste.

8

9

10

11

11   Part of the Royal Arsenal Canal was filled in during the 1920s and 1930s but although no longer navigable, a large part of it was still in existence when I visited the Arsenal in February 1968. The lock was badly silted and the original gates were incapable of holding water. Nothing had been done to preclude the canal's renovation, as the swing bridge over the head of the lock which appeared to be of comparatively recent construction was complete with operating machinery and the canal above, although shallow, was free of obstruction. This section of Woolwich Arsenal was closed and absorbed into the Thamesmead Housing complex, the canal being obliterated.

12   Barges wait in Dartford Creek while the ice thaws in the spring of 1895.

13   The commissioners of the Dartford and Crayford Navigation first approved the idea of constructing a lock on the River Darent in March 1893. They commissioned Mr W. H. Thomas to draw up plans and B. Cooke and Company obtained the contract for construction and after protracted correspondence over the site work started during May 1894. The lock was available for use from 10 July 1895, but was passed on the level except on Neap Tides, as in the case of this sailing barge which passed up through the lock in 1897. The buildings in the background are the *Daily Telegraph* Paper Mills.

12

13

14

15

14 Thames sailing barges on the Dartford & Crayford Navigation, above Dartford Lock about 1910. The barge on the right is being unloaded by steam crane.

15 A sailing barge and lighters outside Phoenix Mills, Dartford, at the head of the Dartford and Crayford Navigation about 1920.

16 The real life 'Peggoty's Boat-house' of Dickensian fame photographed in 1910 from the towpath of the Thames and Medway Canal. The roof is the upturned hull of a boat, and the house lay next to the canal and between it and the Thames marshland. The house was at one time used as a base for hiring out rowing boats.

17 and **18** The Thames and Medway Canal was designed for use by sailing barges, and of course provision was made for their masts. All bridges over the canal were moveable so that the only fixed obstruction to headroom was the tunnel at Higham. The bridges over the entrance locks at Gravesend were both swing bridges, and that over the river lock is still in working order. Of the remaining four bridges, the first out of Gravesend was a swing bridge, as depicted in the photograph, which was taken in 1924. Another more unusual structure, was the Lift Bridge at Mark Lane. The central platform rose vertically, being counterbalanced by the weights that are visible at each corner. Neither of these bridges is now in existence.

19 Although Higham Tunnel was converted to railway use during 1847, the canal from the Thames at Gravesend, as far as Higham (a distance of four miles) was kept open for navigation, although trade continued to decline. The traffic was mainly Manure, bound for the Dung Wharf at Higham with a return cargo of farm produce! This barge has just arrived at the Dung Wharf, and is waiting to be relieved of its cargo of manure about 1920.

20 Higham Tunnel is driven for most of its length through Chalk, with some lengths through Fuller's Earth. The rock is very hard and massive and therefore a considerable proportion of the tunnel was left unlined. The arch was brick-lined where loose chalk was encountered and also a portion either side of the working shafts. Nevertheless, there were accidents due to roof falls, although this was nothing uncommon in a work of such magnitude. The tunnel varied in size slightly according to the irregularities in the rock, but in general, was about 35ft from invert to arch and 26ft 6in from wall to wall including a 5ft towing path.

21 In 1844 it was decided that a railway should be built alongside the canal, and a single track was laid through the tunnel, with one rail on the towing path and the other supported on stantions resting on the canal bed. This enabled the tunnel to be used both for rail and water transport. This print, made in 1845, shows the Frindsbury (or Strood) entrance to the tunnel, and the railway track can clearly be seen curving away to the left from the tunnel mouth.

22 and 23 After the conversion of the tunnel to sole railway use during 1846 and 1847, the basin at Frindsbury was used as a dock. It relied for its water supply on water from the Medway flowing back through the lock, at high tide. Unfortunately, the water took with it a considerable quantity of river silt which periodically had to be cleared. These photographs show dredging in progress during 1905, and the steam dredger loading the sailing barge *Thomas* with spoil. Both the tunnel entrance and the river lock are clearly visible.

22

23

24   During the eighteenth and nineteenth centuries the hulks of old sailing ships were moored on the Medway at Chatham, and used as *Prison Ships* by the Navy, particularly for convicts awaiting transportation to Australia.

25 and **26**   During the early days of cement-making on the Thames and Medway estuaries, the small output of the mills was easily transported by road, but as the industry expanded the use of barges grew, until firms built their own barges, and soon had quite sizeable fleets. Fleets were distinguished by company markings. Peter Brothers at Wouldham — whose works are shown here — had a fleet of about thirty barges, which had black hulls and rails, brown quarter boards and the letter 'P' on their sails. Peters started with *Providence*, which was built in 1823, and their last barge *Edwin* was constructed in 1903.

27 The original tidal lock at Allington was constructed as a result of the Lower Medway Navigation Act of 1792. As depicted in the illustration, this was initially a flash lock, with a weir alongside. It would perhaps be more accurate to describe it as a pair of tidal doors. Subsequently, the Lower Medway was improved elsewhere, and in the late 1840s the company replaced the flash lock with a more conventional pound lock.

28 In 1910 the River Medway passed into public control and between 1911 and 1915, great improvements were carried out throughout the navigation. Allington had been left alone during this period, but during 1937 £18,000 was spent modernising the lock and weir. The opening ceremony was performed by Mr W. S. Morrison, the Minister of Agriculture, on 4 August, and it was hoped that the improvements would particularly overcome the flooding which had become an annual problem.

29

29 Maidstone was the major centre of trade on the Medway. The river banks just downstream of Maidstone Bridge were lined with wharves. On the right of the photograph are Canal Wharf and Albion Wharf, and on the left, Bridge Wharf and the Fairmeadow. The old Maidstone Bridge caused an obstruction to traffic on the river, and on the road which crossed it. In order to help ease the congestion, Sir Joseph Bazalgette began building a new bridge. The first pile was driven in on 1 October 1877, and the new bridge opened on 6 August 1879. In this photograph, taken during construction, the iron girders used in building the new bridge have been erected on the northern (or downstream) side of the old bridge. Old Maidstone Bridge was demolished in 1880.

30 and 31 Just upstream of Maidstone Bridge was College Lock, the first lock on the Upper Medway Navigation. In 1880, the Lower Medway Navigation Company deepened Allington Lock, raising the water levels. College Lock had been partially washed away by floods that year, but the alterations at Allington meant that it finally had to be removed, as it was unnecessary. The paddles on College Lock are of interest, as they are identical to those that may be found today, at Worsfold Gates on the River Wey. Just before World War I Bonthron described them thus: 'The locks, by the way, generally speaking, are rather hard to work, and are handled by a long iron crowbar; we borrowed one from a tugman at the first lock at Allington.' In the second photograph of College Lock, a sailing barge can be seen with its mast lowered, having just passed through the lock on its way to East Farleigh, while another, with its mast up, can be seen approaching the lock, at the top of Lock Meadow. The board on the side of the lock house sets out the scale of tolls on the navigation.

32 One of the principal traffics on the Medway was timber, brought upstream from the London Docks by sailing barge, and unloaded either at Maidstone, as shown here, or at Tonbridge.

33 The lock at East Farleigh is the first above Maidstone. The bridge is very old as it is recorded that Cromwell's men under General Fairfax marched over East Farleigh Bridge, on their way to capture Maidstone, killing 300 Royalists and taking 1,500 prisoners. In the winter of 1909-10 East Farleigh Lock collapsed and finally caused the end of the Upper Medway Navigation Company, which had been in a financially embarrassing position. The river was closed for three months, until a Bill was promoted in Parliament to transfer its control to an independent conservancy, under Kent County Council. The Conservancy took control of the river in June 1911, closing the lower part until 1913 and the upper section to Tonbridge until 1915. The photograph shows the lock before its collapse, with two sailing barges leaving the lock on their way downstream to Maidstone. They are working together as a pair, for towing purposes.

34 On 2 August 1904 The Kaiser Steam Tug Company started towing barges from Yalding to Aylesford with their specially built tug *Keston*. The scheme was very successful, but unfortunately the navigation company failed to pay Kaiser and the debt had to be settled by one of the directors Mr A. Reeve. *Keston* was used again on the river, after navigation was restored on 1 September 1915. In fact *Keston* performed the opening ceremony by towing the barge *Beaver*. The photograph shows *Keston* towing the barge *Kingfisher* downstream, near Tonbridge.

35 Sailing barges loaded with timber wait to unload at Tonbridge Wharf. The last regular commercial traffic to Tonbridge ceased in 1927, but a last attempt to revive trade was made in March 1950, when a tug towed a 200-ton barge to the Gas Works at Tonbridge, to test the feasibility of starting a regular coal traffic. Unfortunately, the idea was abandoned.

The Coastal Waterways

36

36 The ancient town of Rye, standing as it does at the mouth of the Rivers Rother, Tillingham and Brede, is a natural port, and has for centuries been visited by vessels from all over the British Isles. In this photograph of Rye Town Quay, taken in 1910, the foremost boat, with the registration number LT 619, comes from Lowestoft.

37 The Royal Military Canal was level throughout, except for a single lock at Iden, where the canal met the River Rother. Iden Lock was 72ft long and 16ft wide with a pair of flood gates below the bottom gates, to prevent excess water flowing back into the canal. The construction of the lock was started in October 1807, and it was completed and opened in September 1808. The last regular traffic through Iden Lock ceased in 1902, but it was not until 15 December 1909 that the sailing barge *Vulture* owned by Mr J. Terry, and loaded with 27 tons of shingle, was the last boat to pass through. In the early 1960s Iden Lock was repaired by the Kent River Catchment Board, though for water control use, and is not passable for navigation.

38 Unloading a Rye Barge just below Newenden Bridge on the Rother on a bright wintry day, early this century. The length and precarious nature of the way-plank is to be wondered at! Boat shafts have been pushed into the bed of the river and lashed onto the boat, to keep it stationary.

38

39 An empty Rye Barge under full sail tacking on the River Rother in a strong wind. The steerer looks in a very precarious position!

40 and **41** The Brede was navigable for eight miles from Brede Bridge to the River Tillingham near Rye. During the eighteenth century barges took iron ore from Rye to the furnaces at Brede, returning with cargoes of guns. Later, an 18in-gauge tramway ran ¾ mile from Brede Bridge Wharf to the nearby Hastings and St Leonards Waterworks. The Rye Barge *Victoria* is seen here in 1923, unloading coal onto the tramway. Rye Barges were about 45ft long and 12ft wide with a draught of 2ft 9in. They carried about 20 tons. The steam locomotive pulled a train of wagons, each of which, when loaded with coal, weighed 4 tons.

42 Sailing barges by Cliff Bridge, Lewes, on the Sussex River Ouse about 1900.

43 The Sussex Ouse became disused above Lindfield in 1861 and above Lewes in 1868, although the locks were occasionally used until the late 1870s, when they fell into total disrepair. This loaded barge is tied up at Barcombe Oil Mills, by the fourth lock on the navigation, although the actual date of this early photograph is unknown.

44 West Marlands Tunnel at Southampton on the Salisbury and Southampton Canal, was started in 1796. By November of that year, problems were experienced with poor soil which caused sinking, but work proceeded. Unfortunately, when John Rennie inspected the works in March 1798, he could only report on bad workmanship and surveying which had resulted in different lengths of bore not lining up. Hill, the engineer, was ordered to put right the defects, but it is doubtful if he ever did, and indeed the tunnel was never completed. The tunnel was to have been 580yd long, but only about 490yd were dug. The tunnel runs under the City, passing within a few yards of the Civic Centre. In 1975 part of the tunnel collapsed, causing subsidence. Fortunately, before the tunnel was filled in at that point, the opportunity was taken to photograph it.

44

45

45 Catherine Hill Lock, on the River Itchen Navigation, was the highest lock on the river, being just one mile short of Blackbridge Wharf, Winchester. Today, a little masonry remains, and a weir has been constructed where the head of the lock would have been.

The Sea to the Thames

46 Southgate Basin, Chichester, about 1906. Commercial traffic on the Chichester Canal had almost died out by the end of the nineteenth century, only 704 tons being carried in 1898. The last commercial trade was in 1906, when Combe's of Bosham carried shingle from Chichester Harbour in a sailing barge, to Southgate Basin. Here, the barge can be seen being unloaded with the help of the hand operated wharf crane. Chichester Cathedral can be seen in the background.

47 and **48** The Portsmouth and Arundel Canal from Hunston to Ford was finally abandoned when the company was wound up in 1896. From that date forward, sections of the canal were filled in. This painting shows the locks, bridge and pumping station at Ford as they were when the canal was in operation. The locks were filled in during the early part of this century, although the bridge remained (photograph No 48) until the 1930s, when it was demolished.

49 A three-masted coasting vessel tied up on the Arun. This photograph was taken by Edward Fox, who died in 1875.

50 A loaded sailing barge approaches Arundel about 1900.

51

51 Bargemaster Henry Doick owned two barges which he worked on the Arun Navigation. This photograph of his barge No 64 was taken below Pulborough Bridge, around 1885. By 1887 Doick's barges were the only ones left on the Arun Navigation, and the navigation was going bankrupt. Notices were issued that the canal would be closed from 1 January 1888, but the canal remained open to any traffic that arrived, and Henry Doick continued trading, until on 20 June 1888, he left Houghton, carrying his last load of chalk: 10 tons for Lee Farm, near Middle Lock, and 20 tons bound for Newbridge.

52 Commercial traffic on the Wey and Arun Canal ceased in 1871; thus illustrations of it in use are, to my knowledge, nonexistent. This photograph shows Rowner Lock (the first on the canal at the Arun end) as it was about 1900, thirty years after navigation ceased. Rowner Lock has now been restored by the Wey and Arun Canal Trust, as part of their attempt to re-open the canal.

53 Sailing barge being unloaded at Elkins Coal Wharf, Guildford, on the Wey Navigation. The photograph has been taken from the High Street Bridge, during the nineteenth century, and at this end of the wharf, just behind Elkins's name board, can be seen the famous tread-mill crane, with its jib swung inland.

52

53

54   These days, dredging is
carried out with quite sophisti-
cated machinery. Before diesel
driven dredgers, there were steam
dredgers, but before that man had
to depend upon his own labours.
The River Wey has always
remained a little backward, so we
are fortunate to see this fine
example of spoon dredging above
Guildford in 1922. The long shaft
is used to balance the weight of
the metal 'spoon' with its load of
spoil.

54

55 Originally, the River Wey Locks were built with sloping turf sides, being similar to a natural length of river simply enclosed by gates at either end. Gradually, over the years they have been converted to a more convenient design. In this photograph taken in May 1907, Paper Court Lock is being converted from turf sided to timber sided, the lock cut having been drained from Worsfold Gates at Send, to below the lock. Paper Court Lock has since been reconstructed again, and is now concrete sided.

55

56 This photograph shows Newark Lock being converted from turf sided to concrete sided in May 1965.

57 Wey Barges belonging to William Stevens and Sons, head upstream towards Newark, in arctic conditions. The smoke is from a cabin stove, a very welcome comfort in such cold weather.

58 A Wey barge nudges the top gates of Pyrford Lock, and the horses feed while waiting for the water to make a level. The building in the background is The Anchor, rather a different establishment in 1955 from the modernised public house that we can visit today. Horsedrawn traffic on the River Wey ceased above Coxes Lock shortly after this.

59 The narrow boat *Alton* belonging to the Narrow Boat Trust, tied up outside The Anchor, just below Pyrford Lock in January 1978. *Alton* had loaded coalite at Gopsall Wharf, on the Ashby de la Zouch Canal, in the Midlands, for delivery to properties alongside the River Wey. Regular commercial traffic to Guildford ceased in 1958; in 1970 the narrow boat *Jaguar*, took a load of coal to Godalming as part of the Inland Waterways Association's National Rally of Boats. *Alton* was the first commercial craft to reach Guildford since then. *Alton* was built for the Grand Union Canal Carrying Company in 1937, by Harland & Wolff at Woolwich, and is a Town Class narrow boat.

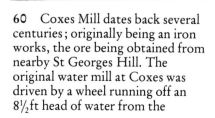

60 Coxes Mill dates back several centuries; originally being an iron works, the ore being obtained from nearby St Georges Hill. The original water mill at Coxes was driven by a wheel running off an $8\frac{1}{2}$ ft head of water from the $7\frac{1}{2}$-acre mill pond. Today the wheel drives a 50hp electric generator. Most of the mill buildings are fairly modern but parts date back to about 1829. Here we see sacks of grain being unloaded from a barge during the 1860s.

61

61 The West Country barge *Perseverance* half unloaded at Coxes Mill in 1885. *Perseverance* was built at Honey Street on the Kennet and Avon Canal, by Robin Lane and Pinnegar. Her last skipper was Bill Hickman of Weybridge, who died in 1968. Barge traffic to Coxes Mill from London Docks continued until July 1969, when William Stevens and Sons were forced to cease trading, with the removal of the grain terminals to Tilbury Docks. Last barges on the 'grain run', were *Hope*, *Speedwell* and *Perseverance IV* (not the barge shown in the photograph). In the autumn of 1978 the traffic was revived by Tam and Di Murrell, who are transhipping the grain from barge to narrow boats at Shepperton on the Thames, for the last 2 miles up the Wey to Coxes Mill.

62 The Basingstoke Barge *Red Jacket* passes under Black Boy Bridge above Town Lock on the River Wey. *Red Jacket* was built by Costains of Berkhamstead on the Grand Junction Canal in 1909, for A. J. Harmsworth. It was of wooden construction 72ft 6in long, 13ft 2in beam and 5ft 2in in the side. It carried 70 tons of coal under hatches below Weybridge and 50 tons of round timber down from Crookham in World War I. *Red Jacket* was rebuilt at Ash Vale in the late 1920s and sold in 1940, to carry explosives up the River Lee to Waltham Abbey Explosives Works. It was lost in an air raid, while so employed.

63 An unknown barge, heavily loaded with timber, passes upstream under Black Boy Bridge. One of the problems with timber, on the River Wey, was that barges either travelled half empty or loaded to capacity, and risked delays at the low bridges. The skipper of this barge must have been an expert!

64 The narrow boat *Basingstoke* loaded with coal and tied up above Thames Lock on the Wey. Weybridge Oil Mills can be seen in the background: Linseed was carried here by barge, until the mill was burnt down in 1963. *Basingstoke* is believed to have been built at Appledore in North Devon during the 1870s. In the 1880s it was owned by the Woking, Aldershot and Basingstoke Canal Navigation Company, and sold in 1893 to the Nately Brick and Tile Company for carrying their products to Ash Wharf, to Basingstoke and to other wharves along the canal. In 1907 they sold it to A. J. Harmsworth who used it as a lightening boat, to carry sand, round timber and coal, particularly to Woking Gas Works. Between 1912 and 1914 Alec Harmsworth used *Basingstoke* in his historic attempt to delay abandonment of the western end of the Basingstoke Canal, by navigating its full length. In 1933 *Basingstoke* was taken to Ash Vale, and its iron frames were removed and used to build the barge *Brookwood*. Its remains can still be seen in Great Bottom Flash.

65

66

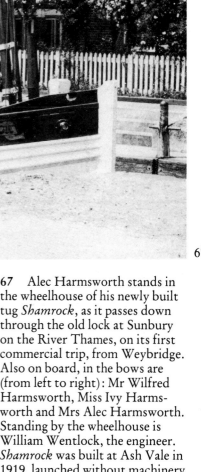

65 The William Stevens barge *Hope* passes up through Thames Lock on the River Wey in 1951. Skipper Stan Ellis is on the barge, while mate Len Turner stands on the bank. Horse towage on the River Wey continued until 1960.

66 Here, *Hope* is seen waiting below Thames Lock in the pound above the flash lock (or flood gates). Craft entering the River Wey from the River Thames pause above the flood gates while they are closed, and water is let down from above to enable them to pass over the bottom cill of Thames Lock, which otherwise has a mere 18in of water over it.

67 Alec Harmsworth stands in the wheelhouse of his newly built tug *Shamrock*, as it passes down through the old lock at Sunbury on the River Thames, on its first commercial trip, from Weybridge. Also on board, in the bows are (from left to right): Mr Wilfred Harmsworth, Miss Ivy Harmsworth and Mrs Alec Harmsworth. Standing by the wheelhouse is William Wentlock, the engineer. *Shamrock* was built at Ash Vale in 1919, launched without machinery and taken to Tom Taylor's yard at Staines to be fitted out. Cast iron billets had to be loaded into her to get the head down, as the hull floated too high in the water to get under the bridges. She was finished in early summer 1920. Behind *Shamrock* is *Josephine*, a wooden barge built at Ash Vale in 1919, 73ft 6in long, with 13ft 10½in beam, and capable of carrying 95 tons.

68

69

68 The Basingstoke Barge *Gwendoline* is pulled out of Scotland Lock, in the Woodham Flight, en route to Woking Gasworks loaded with 40-50 tons of coal, in 1934. *Gwendoline* was built at Ash Vale as a resident barge in 1921, by A. J. Harmsworth, who used her for trading. She was sold in 1950.

69 'Digging out' below lock 9 at St John's (Goldsworth) on the Basingstoke Canal in 1912. Digging out the flight was all done by hand and was spread over a period of three years.

70 Barge building at Ash Vale started in 1918 with *Rosaline* and continued with about one barge a year being built, until it finished with *Ariel I* in 1935. With the exception of *Aldershot*, seen here under construction, and launched in 1932, all barges were built on the northern side of the canal, while repair work was carried out opposite on the land now occupied by the Surrey and Hampshire Canal Society. All barges were 72ft 6in long and 13ft 10½in wide, but the height in the side varied from 5ft to 6ft. The bottoms were of 2½in-thick pine with 1in deal sheathing inside, while the chines, sides and frames were of oak. The last barge to be repaired at Ash Vale was *Perseverance* in 1947, and in 1959 the barge business was sold, shortly after the canal.

71 In 1913, as part of a legal battle to keep the canal open, Alec Harmsworth was persuaded by William Carter, then holding the Basingstoke Canal as mortgagee, to attempt to get a boat along the entire length of the canal. Harmsworth made the attempt, in the narrow boat *Basingstoke*, and reached Basing Wharf in December 1913, where he turned back after receiving a telegram from Carter to say that the battle had been won. Here Alec Harmsworth (standing on the cabin), is seen forcing a passage through the reeds between Nateley and the Little Tunnel. This was the last time a boat reached as far as this.

72 A narrow boat unloads coal at Odiham Great Wharf in 1867.

72

Around the Thames

73, 74 and 75 The river lock where MacMurray's Canal meets the River Thames upstream of Wandsworth Bridge was the only lock on the canal; the buildings in the background are the Southwark and Vauxhall Waterworks. The canal became disused about 1920, and was eliminated in the 1930s in two stages: first the section from the Thames as far as the Llangollen Canal-style lift bridge shown in the second photograph, between 1932 and 1937; and secondly, from there to the head of navigation behind Young and Co's Ram Brewery, by 1940. Here, malt barges can be seen tied up at the Brewery Wharf. These photographs were taken about 1910.

76

77

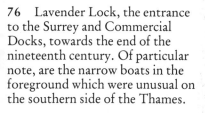

76 Lavender Lock, the entrance to the Surrey and Commercial Docks, towards the end of the nineteenth century. Of particular note, are the narrow boats in the foreground which were unusual on the southern side of the Thames.

77 The directors of the Surrey and Commercial Docks Company pose for the photographer, towards the end of the nineteenth century.

78 and 79 Canada Dock under construction. Firstly, the entrance from (probably) Albion Dock, being dug out by hand, surrounded by steam cranes. The dock itself was excavated by hand too, but a steam tramway took away the spoil, thus obviating the need for lengthy barrow runs.

80 The only lock on the Grand Surrey Canal was where boats locked down out of Greenland Dock, into the canal. Here, in 1949, a train of timber lighters is gradually being passed through the lock, with the help of a small tug.

81 Timber was the principal traffic, both on the Grand Surrey Canal, and in the Surrey Docks, where ships from North America and Scandinavia landed their cargoes or transhipped them into canal barges or lighters. The canal was lined with wharves, where timber merchants received and stored their stocks. This photograph, taken in 1949, shows just two of the timber wharves, with lighters waiting to unload.

81

82 Sailing barges load refuse from the dust chutes on the Grand Surrey Canal near the Old Kent Road in 1920.

83 The heavily laden sailing barge *Ivy* tied up at St Georges Bridge, near the Camberwell terminus of the Grand Surrey Canal in 1925.

84 and **85** The Kensington Canal was tidal all the way from the Thames to its lock, which was situated by what is now the Cromwell Road. In these pictures, taken in 1902, we can see the contrast between high and low tide. Vigers Wharf was situated just south of the Kings Road.

84

85

86 This unusual photograph taken in October 1903 shows a pair of horsedrawn narrow boats on the mud at low tide on the Kensington Canal beside the partly constructed Lots Road Power Station. The forecabin as on *Elizabeth* was a common sight at the time and provided the family with extra accommodation for two children.

87 Not actually part of a canal — but a new dock under construction at the entrance to the Kensington Canal, by Lots Road Power Station, about 1900-10. Of particular interest is the chute on the right for conveying the vast number of bricks required to line the bottom of the dock.

88 Chelsea Waterworks, set up by Act of Parliament in 1721 was a forerunner in its field. Situated on marshy land next to the Thames, it was able to use the streams flowing through the area as a form of reservoir. These streams, used also for navigation as depicted in this print of 1752, were the predecessors of the Grosvenor Canal. Note the two Newcomen steam pumping engines on the left.

87

88

89 As can be seen in this photograph of 1885, the original Grosvenor Canal lock house was a very grandiose affair. What is more, how many lock-keepers today would go to work in a white shirt, black bow tie, waistcoat and bowler hat?

90 By early 1928 the Grosvenor Canal had passed from the Duke of Westminster's control, and had spent over twenty years under Westminster City Council. Somehow, that fact shows in the atmosphere conveyed in this illustration of the lock. Note the gas lamp, the slight influx of concrete and the utilitarian looking building on the right. The lock would take craft up to 90ft × 18ft 6in and drawing about 7ft 6in.

91 The Grosvenor Canal in 1928, looking north from the entrance lock towards Ebury Bridge, which can be seen in the distance. The first sailing barge, on the left, is from Rochester.

92 and **93** In July 1928 the Grosvenor Canal was closed for a year for the lock to be completely rebuilt and the canal bed above to be dug out square and lined with concrete. The size of the lock was increased to 140ft long by 25ft 4in wide, but the length of the canal from the head of the lock to its terminus was reduced from 437yd to merely 163yd. The scheme was engineered by Mr G. J. Griffiths, engineer to the Thames Conservancy, and the work, costing £85,172 13s 0d was carried out by L. J. Speight Ltd. The work entailed the excavation of 26,000 tons of material, and the use of 22,400 tons of mass concrete and 380 tons of steel piling.

94 The Grosvenor Canal was re-opened to navigation on 3 July 1929, by Major Vivian Rogers, the Mayor of Westminster. Since then, it has been used solely by West-minster City Council, and their contractors Cory Lighterage, for barging refuse to the Thames marshes.

95 Beam Bridge Lock, on the incomplete Romford Canal in 1937. About three miles of the canal was constructed but none of it was ever opened as the river lock was never completed. Beam Bridge Lock merely awaited bottom gates and paddle gearing, but work stopped and the company was wound up before this could happen. The lock and this section of the canal have been filled in for some years.

96 Rainham Road Bridge was the next above Beam Bridge Lock, and never had any water beneath it. During World War II the arch was blocked up and used as a pill-box, but following the war the bridge was completely removed.

97 This bascule bridge carried a tramway over the River Roding from 1903 until 1929. A local inhabitant described their memories of it thus: '... the bell would ring and then we would see this massive structure divide into halves and go up to let the boats through. Even now, I can imagine I hear the final bang of the two parts fitting together again after the boats have gone through, and see everyone scampering across the bridge like a lot of rats.'

98 Barking Mill, 1869. There has been a watermill on the Roding at Barking since the time of the Domesday Book, although the first time the site is recorded is on a map of 1653. It is thought that steam power was installed during the 1850s, but certainly when this photograph was taken, T. D. Ridley and Sons who owned the mill were using both steam and water power. In this view of the mill, the eighteenth-century mill house can clearly be seen on the right. The mill and mill house were demolished in 1922. On the extreme left of the photograph can be seen the entrance to Barking Flash Lock.

Town Quay, Barking

99

100

99 The existence of a wharf on the site of Barking Town Quay dates back to the founding of the nearby abbey in the seventh century. The wharf was owned by the abbey and used by boats bringing provisions, and for carrying corn and meal to and from the adjoining watermill. The wharf remained important, initially with the growth of Barking as a fishing port, and subsequently in the nineteenth century, when the growth of market gardening led to an increase in the demand for manure. With the increase in emphasis placed on road transport, the importance of the creek and town quay to the economy of the area has declined. This photograph shows the town quay in 1900.

100 Jackson and Co were builders' merchants and here in this photograph from 1910 they are receiving building materials which are being unloaded from the sailing barge on the left. The ends of Factory Street and Emily Cottages can be seen behind the barges on the right, which are loaded with coal possibly bound for Barking Gas Works, one of whose gas-holders towers above the houses in the background.

101 and 102 Horse drawn barges squeeze past each other near the head of navigation on the River Stort, at Bishops Stortford, about 1900. The river was at that time in a poor state of repair, much work being required on the locks, as can be seen at this turf sided lock at South Mills. Unfortunately nothing was done until the river was sold to the Lee Conservancy Board. The sale took place in 1911, repairs were started in 1913, and completed (including reconstructing the locks) on 4 July 1924. Commercial traffic was briefly revived, but died away immediately following World War II.

103 Dickers Mill at Hertford used the River Lee extensively, both for carrying grain to the mill, and for carrying flour away. Here, about 1900, a sailing barge has just finished unloading.

104 Until the Lee Conservancy Act of 1868, navigation on the river had been administered by Trustees. After the Act, the Lee Conservancy Board was established, taking over control of the river from the first Friday in April 1869. The Conservancy Board carried out an annual inspection of their navigation, aboard their steam barge *Salisbury*. Here they are posing for the photographer before setting out on their inspection in 1892.

104

105 and **106** On 17 July 1922, a massive reconstruction of the Lee Navigation was started. Nine locks between Enfield and Hertford were rebuilt, their width being increased from 13ft 3in to 16ft and their length to 90ft. Also, new bridges were built at Enfield Lock and Waltham Abbey, with the towing path running under the bridge rather than round it. The work cost about £100,000, and was completed by mid-June 1923. In photograph 105 we can see a traction engine driving a pump to keep the works dry at Waltham Town Lock, and photograph 106 shows another lock, with the area alongside the old chamber excavated ready for the widening of the lock to start.

105

106

107

107 Bow hauling an empty lighter into one of the enlarged locks on the River Lee. The new gates fitted during the reconstruction had balance beams to open them, unlike those before, which had to be moved with a long shaft.

108 and **109** Limehouse Lock, where the Limehouse Cut joined the tidal Thames was of very strange construction. Like all the pre-1922 Lee Locks, there were no balance beams and the lock walls were timbered. Limehouse Lock was different in that due to subsidence the sides of the lock had to be held apart with wooden braces, giving the lock the appearance of having a roof. However, by 1967 the lock was falling further and further into a state of dis-

repair, so that the British Waterways Board decided to cut a new length of canal from Limehouse Cut into the adjacent Regent's Canal Dock. The scheme was described as '. . . an alternative to reconstructing Limehouse Lock, which was built many years ago and is now in poor condition. There is not enough land available to build a new lock by the side of the old one — and to close it for a year to reconstruct it would mean loss of traffic.'

108

110 The Bow Back Rivers have always been a problem in times of flood. They have dual uses, as drainage channels and navigable cuts. The basic problem was that due to the complex nature of the channels, there was no fast through passage for flood water, which thus backed up. With new powers obtained in 1929 and 1930, the Lee Conservancy Board and the local councils embarked on a joint scheme to improve the situation. A main drainage channel was formed of the Waterworks River and the Three Mills River. Two new locks were constructed to connect the navigable channels to this main drainage channel. City Mills Lock, seen here in 1967, and already derelict, was the southern-most junction and joined the Bow Back River (above the lock) with the main drain. City Mills Lock replaced the former Marsh Gate Lock, and was constructed by Messrs John Mowlem and Company Ltd.

111 Carpenters Road Lock, again seen here in 1967, was the other new lock, and formed the northern junction and joined the Old River Lee and the City Mills River to the Waterworks River.

The lock was fitted with radial gates of steel, while the chamber was of mass concrete. It was built by Messrs John Gill, Contractors Ltd.

The Long Distance Route to the North

112

112 Ships throng the waters of
the Regent's Canal Dock in June
1908. Sail was still the predomi-
nant motive power, although
funnels were beginning to appear.

113 A pair of Star Class boats of the Grand Union Canal Carrying Company load drums over the side in the Regent's Canal Dock at Limehouse, while dwarfed by the bows of the ship. The loading is done by dockers, while the boatman and his wife look on.

114 Four Fellows, Morton and Clayton pairs of narrow boats cluster around a ship in the Regent's Canal Dock in the early 1930s. Three pairs have their holds clear, cloths neatly rolled, and wait their turn beneath the hoist. *Penguin* has loosed off its butty which is being loaded under the watchful eye of the boatman's wife.

115 Waiting for the ship to arrive: eight pairs of narrow boats, from both the Fellows, Morton and Clayton, and the Associated Canal Carriers fleets wait to load in the Regent's Canal Dock at Limehouse in 1933. Associated Canal Carriers was the carrying company belonging to the Grand Union Canal Company; it changed its name to the Grand Union Canal Carrying Company in June 1934. On the outside of the string are the Royalty Class pair *Edward* (motor) and *Alexandra* (butty with forecabin); next is the motor *Josephine Marguerite*, probably with its butty *Coombe Abbey*; then the Royalty Class pair *Henry* (motor) and *Anne* (butty — with forecabin). The Royalty Class boats were ordered by Associated Canal Carriers in February 1931. The motors were of steel construction and were built at Yarwoods of Northwich and Pollocks of Faversham, while the butties were wooden and came from Walkers of Rickmansworth, Woods of Brentford and Bushell Brothers of Tring. They were the largest narrow boats on the canals, being 4ft 11in in the side. In the middle of the string can be seen the wooden Fellows, Morton and Clayton motor boat *Swallow* which was built at that company's yard at Uxbridge in 1925, at a cost of £600. By the side of the dock is the ex-Steamer *Baron*. *Baron* was a purpose built steamer of iron composite construction launched in November 1898 at Fellows, Morton and Clayton's yard at Saltley, Birmingham. It had elm bottoms, a pitch pine keelson and wrought iron sides. Its engine was built by Nettlefolds of Birmingham and boiler by Fletchers of Derby. In February/March 1915 *Baron* was the first of the steamers to be converted to a motor boat, with a 15hp Bolinder semi-diesel engine from Sweden. The engine cost £157 and the other conversion costs amounted to another £244.

116 Large chunks of the Grand Union Canal Carrying Company's fleet were often used to clear an entire ship in one go. Here in 1937, a mixture of Town Class and Star Class narrow boats — eleven pairs in all — have loaded and clothed up and await customs clearance before starting the long haul towards Birmingham.

116

117, 118, 119 and **120** Following the success of the Royalty Class narrow boats, the Grand Union Canal Carrying Company placed orders for six wooden pairs of smaller boats, which became the forerunners of the Star Class. These prototypes were followed by batch orders:

January 1935 24 pairs iron sides/ elm bottoms, from Harland & Wolff
January 1935 12 pairs iron sides/ elm bottoms, from Yarwoods
January 1935 6 pairs oak sides/ elm bottoms, from Walkers
May 1935 18 pairs steel sides/elm bottoms, from Harland & Wolff
May 1935 8 pairs all steel with vee bottoms, from Yarwoods
May 1935 12 pairs oak sides/elm bottoms, from Walkers
May 1935 2 pairs all wood, from Woods

The first batch of boats from Harland and Wolff at Woolwich on the Thames, started being delivered in May 1935. The initial two pairs were *Themis* and *Titania*, and *Hyperion* and *Hyades*. These four photographs show this first batch in various stages of construction. Firstly, the sterns of three motors can be seen with counter rolls, counter plate, cabin bulkhead and shafting in position. Swim plates have been fitted to the hull on the far side. In the background, a completed motor boat is being hoisted onto the slipway ready for launching. Meanwhile, in the sheds, a nearly completed pair is being dressed. The motor boat's propeller is being balanced and on the sides of its cabin can be seen the signwriter's chalk marks, his work at this stage being incomplete. The ram's head on the butty is up on wedges and is being hung. In the third photograph an almost completed motor boat is being moved, possibly into the sheds, for dressing up. Finally, the first motor boat, *Themis* is pulled down the slip into the river. The exhaust funnel above the engine room was a feature that was later to be replaced with a more conventional stack.

117

118

119

120

121 A horse drawn coal barge enters Mile End Lock on the Regent's Canal on its way up from the docks in 1954.

122 A Regent's Canal barge horse pauses for a feed. The ear cosy fulfilled two functions: warmth and keeping the flies away, hence the tufts.

123 Two Pickford's narrow boats leave City Road Lock on their way from London Docks, possibly to the company's Manchester base. The boat on the left is towed out of the lock towards the 960yd Islington Tunnel by two men. The other boat is to receive the same treatment, while the horse is taken across the hill to meet the boats at the other end.

124 The lighter *Tuber* is unloaded just above Hampstead Road Lock on the Regent's Canal. Lighter traffic up the canal had been declining for years and has now ceased. The trade in timber to the top of the locks, seen here in 1969, was about the last. This small basin is now a recreation area, with craft shops and restaurants.

125 Jason's Trip was started by John James in 1951, as his contribution to Festival of Britain Year. John ran trips from Maida Hill Tunnel to the Hampstead Road and back using *Jason*, a Samuel Barlow boat, which had originally been commissioned for the carrying firm Nelson's. Here, on 8 August 1952, *Jason* is about to enter Regents Park on the return trip. The boat is being steered by his father Jack James, while John, wearing a dark suit, sits with his passengers, giving a commentary. In 1958 the original *Jason* was replaced by a steel boat from Thomas Clayton's of Oldbury, and joined in 1968 by the butty *Serpens*. John sold the business in 1972, *Jason*'s twenty-first year, and it is still operating. Jason's Trip was largely responsible for the development of the Regent's Canal for leisure use in the way we know it today.

124

126 Macclesfield Bridge is situated in the cutting through which the Regent's Canal traverses Regents Park. At the time that Thomas Homer was building the canal — and the stretch through Regents Park was part of the first section of the canal to be built — Nash was laying out his plans for the Park itself. Thus, Macclesfield Bridge — named after the canal company's chairman — was very ornamental, with Doric columns and cast iron railings. It was hoped that the bridge would enhance rather than detract from the surroundings of the park.

127 On the morning of Friday 2 October 1874 at about 3am, the steam tug *Ready* left City Road Basin with a train of five barges — *Jane, Dee, Tilbury* and two others. *Tilbury*, captained by Charles Baxton from Loughborough had general cargo on board, including sugar, nuts, strawboards, tea, two or three barrels of petroleum and about five tons of gunpowder from the Arsenal at Woolwich. A few minutes before 5am, as *Ready* passed under Macclesfield Bridge, a spark from its chimney landed on the deck of *Tilbury*, setting alight some loose gunpowder. As *Tilbury* passed under the bridge she blew up, demolishing it and sinking one of the other barges. The explosion could be heard up to 12 miles away and the windows of buildings in the vicinity were smashed. The obstruction to the canal was removed by 6 October. *Tilbury* was owned by the Grand Junction Canal Company, so that the responsibility for rebuilding the bridge fell to them. The original Doric columns were re-used, as is shown by the fact that they were placed the other way round, leaving the grooves caused by the horse tow ropes on the side away from the canal.

128 A train of lighters carrying coal and timber pass through the cutting in Regents Park in 1935 towed by a steam tug. The tow path along this section of the Regent's Canal is now open to the public as a canal-side walk.

129 Following *Jason*'s success, Lord St Davids started running longer trips in the *Evelyn*, towing the boat part way by tractor and part way by horse. Here, in 1953, Lord St Davids is driving the tractor along the towpath towards Little Venice, from Maida Hill Tunnel, which can be seen in the background.

130 Paddington Basin on the Paddington Arm of the Grand Junction Canal, still in use commercially in 1935. Wide boats on the left have been loaded with refuse, and await collection by a tug. On the right the wide boat *Shamrock* is loaded with scrap metal.

131 and **132** Paddington Basin was closed for cleaning during April 1909, all of which had to be done by hand, with shovels and wheelbarrows. This gang is working at No 14 North Wharf, while at the other end of the cut to the basin, in Little Venice, a vast array of both loaded and empty narrow boats and wide boats wait for the work to be completed. The boats belonged to a large number of small carrying firms, such as James Nixon of Northolt, that are unknown today.

131

132

133

133 On 27 September 1930, the barge *Elsdale* arrived at Little Venice, Paddington for a dedication service by the Bishop of Bermuda. *Elsdale* had been converted for use as a floating school for canal children at Bulls Bridge, Southall.

134 A number of loaded wide boats wait for towage early one morning in April 1909. 'Paddington Stop', the gauging point where the Regent's Canal met the Paddington Arm of the Grand Junction Canal is in the distance to the right.

135 Wedlake Street Footbridge (off the Harrow Road) is seen here on 4 May 1905 under construction. Locally it was known as 'Ha'penny Steps' because a toll of one half penny was originally charged for every person passing over it. An old man used to tell how, when he was a child, his father carried him over the bridge in a sack to avoid paying for two people.

136 The Fellows, Morton and Clayton steamer *Victory* and butty, pass a horsedrawn maintenance flat on the Paddington Arm of the Grand Junction Canal, just before World War I. *Victory* was built in 1911 at Saltley, of iron composite construction and was converted to a motor boat in August 1927.

137 Steam tugs like this one (seen near Kensal Green Gas Works in February 1931) owned by Charrington, Gardner Locket Co Ltd, were in extensive use towing trains of wide boats and lighters on the Paddington Arm of the Grand Junction Canal.

138

139

138 H. Sabey and Co, a small carrying concern based in Paddington would have used a similar tug — or a diesel powered one — to pull this train of wide boats carrying refuse to Brentford from Paddington.

139 One such tug was the *Fasnet*, seen here with crew (from left to right) Harry Blant, Bill Sculley and Freddy Cave. *Fasnet* was powered by a water-cooled diesel engine.

140 Sabey also ran a number of horsedrawn narrow boats. Here *Orient* and *Empress* are tied up on the Paddington Arm. In the foreground can be seen a horse nose bowl, and on the wharf on the opposite side of the canal, the upturned traces of horse carts.

141

The canal.
northolt. 7.

142

143

141 The wide boat *Pelican*, just unloaded at Alperton Wharf on the Paddington Arm about 1923. Another boat waits to unload, while a train of wide boats passes heading towards Bulls Bridge.

142 A Grand Junction Canal Company maintenance gang pose for the camera with their horse-drawn mud hopper, near Northolt, about 1920.

144

143 The Paddington Packet Boat ran between Paddington and Uxbridge, carrying passengers and parcels from 1801 until about 1806. It was famous, in its time, and the crew were required by the Grand Junction Canal Company, to wear a distinctive uniform: '... the steersman of the passage boat be provided with a Blue Waterman's Jacket with yellow stand-up cape and a double row of yellow buttons — and that the Postillions be also provided with Blue Jackets with Yellow stand-up capes and plain yellow buttons and to have yellow badges on the left arm with the letters G.J.C. thereon.'

144 A. & G. Jupp's Sailing Barge *Alfred* in Brentford Draw Dock, her hull just having been 'blacked' with pitch about 1893.

145 The horsedrawn barge *Frays* leaves Brentford Gauging Lock in November 1945. *Frays* has left the lock, which can be seen to the left of the picture and is using the flow from the River Brent to travel under the High Street Bridge to the next section of towpath.

145

146 A loaded pair of horseboats
squeeze past an assortment of
narrowboats and lighters, as they
are slowly pulled into Brentford
gauging lock in the early 1890s.
Unlike the narrow boat chimneys
of later years, no brass bands can
be seen round those in the picture.

147 and **148** There have been three sets of locks at Brentford. The original lock was a normal single Grand Junction Canal lock, with a brick hump-back bridge over its tail. It is depicted here in 1893. Unfortunately, both the lock and bridge were washed away in floods in 1898. They were replaced by a pair of locks of more modern design, which were themselves later modernised.

149 The modernised Brentford Gauging Lock, following a period of record rainfall in June 1903. The line of the canal curves round to the left in front of the moored lighters.

150 The wide boat *Golden Spray*, having just loaded heads towards the tail of Brentford Gauging Lock about 1935. The girl standing halfway down the hold has paused while clothing up. *Golden Spray* was built by Bushell Brothers of Tring, and displays the excellence of their painting. The boat belonged to T. W. Toovey of Kings Langley.

151

152

151 A loaded lighter enters Brentford Dock, having locked up onto the Grand Union Canal from the River Thames. An empty lighter, having discharged its cargo, is shafted towards the lock to start its journey back to the London Docks. Brentford Gauging Lock has since been modernised and is operated electrically.

152 The wooden horsedrawn narrow boat *Stockport* lies on its side in Brentford Weigh Dock. Here, on 27 May 1910, an attempt is being made to set the boat the right way up in order to refloat it.

153 Fellows, Morton and Clayton horseboats *Surrey* and *Walnut* having loaded, are tied up near Brentford before heading for the north. The photograph is almost certainly posed, but does show the traditional style of dress in use on the canals around 1910.

153

154

155

154 Brentford Dock in 1950 — organised chaos reigns! An empty lighter passes amidst a number of narrow boats, both loaded and empty. The Town Class butty *Ayr* was built in 1936 by Harland and Wolff at Woolwich, for the Grand Union Canal Carrying Company. Although the GUCCC fleet had by this time been nationalised along with the waterway, *Ayr* still sports pre-nationalisation livery. *Ayr* is being loaded with cargo from the lighter on the left of the photograph.

155 Lighter traffic used the bottom part of the Grand Union Canal quite extensively, mainly for local distribution and collection of goods and conveyance to the docks. Here in June 1955 a horse-drawn lighter loaded with timber approaches Brentford.

156 Brentford 'dock' in 1954, was still a major transhipment point for goods destined for the north. At that time, it was in the control of British Transport Waterways, a division of the Docks and Inland Waterways

Executive of the British Transport Commission. The butty *Barnes* was built in steel in 1936 by Harland and Wolff at Woolwich for the Grand Union Canal Carrying Co. The butty *Streatham* was a wooden boat, built by Walkers of Rickmansworth in 1936, and the unknown motor between them was built by Yarwoods of Northwich. All three are Town Class boats.

157 *Bristol* and *Branksome* leave
Brentford in June 1955, heavily
laden, with cloths tied down tight-
ly, ready for the long climb up the
Chilterns that lies ahead. The
boatman's wife is steering, while he
tightens the straps that keep the
pair of boats breasted up. Both
boats were built in 1936 for the
GUCCC by Harland and Wolff at
Woolwich.

158 A Grand Junction Canal
Company maintenance gang
involved in bricklaying in 1896, at a
lock just above Brentford.

158

159   This train of wideboats and
their tug were stuck in the ice
above Hanwell for some days
during the winter of 1933. At least
the occupants of *Penguin* were able
to keep warm by using some of
their cargo of coal!

160

161

160, 161 and **162** These photographs show maintenance stoppages in the busy years of canal transport. The differences apparent between the organisation then and now are quite outstanding. Timing was critical, and designed solely to restrict traffic movement as little as possible. All three pictures depict work on Hanwell Locks on the Grand Junction Canal. The first two on a Summer Sunday in 1909 — work involving draining the lock and raising the gates, which would today take a couple of weeks. The third photo-graph shows similar work carried out over Whitsun weekend in 1911. The concept involved a heavy injection of labour and materials for a short space of time, rather than the current method of employing a small gang of men with the bare necessities over a longer period. To the canal company, loss of toll revenue due to delayed traffic was a major consideration so work took place when boat movement was at its least. Today with the vast majority of waterway users being at leisure, stoppages take place during the week over the winter months; unfortunately this totally disrupts the little commercial traffic which remains and discourages potential trade in a climate where carriers are unable to guarantee continuity of traffic due to the length of stoppages, the siting of coincidental stoppages and the unpredictability of unplanned work. Due to the modern annual licence method of collecting revenue the duration of stoppages no longer hits the canal management's finances as it used to, so priorities have changed.

163 The Grand Junction Canal at Norwood, stopped off while a gas main is laid across the bed, early this century. The mill next to the bridge was destroyed by fire in 1912.

164 A heavily laden horsedrawn day boat passes under a bridge near North Hyde on the Grand Junction Canal about 1905.

164

165   Cleaning out the bed of the Grand Junction Canal underneath a bridge at Hayes. The work is believed to have been in connection with bridge modernisation in May 1934.

166 *Pioneer* was an experimental motorised wide boat, built by Fellows, Morton and Clayton at their dock at Uxbridge and seen here just after launching in October 1934. *Pioneer* was intended to cut down crew numbers on the trade to John Dickinson's Paper Mill, but was found too wide to keep to the tight schedule required. The boat was sold in about 1938 to the Harefield Lime Company at Springwell. The dock staff posing on *Pioneer* are, from left to right: Harry Hough (fitter); Len Hough (fitter and son of Harry); George Bristow (blacksmith's mate); Ezra James (boatbuilder); Harry Penn (boatbuilder — responsible for most of the painting); Arthur Penn (boatbuilder and son of Harry); Reg Kempton (boatbuilder); Harry J. Crook (boatbuilder); Harry Crook (boat-builder and yard foreman); and Arthur Chambers (boatbuilder). *Pioneer* was built on the same lines and to the same specifications as an ordinary narrow boat, but about 12ft 6in wide. It was left to Harry Crook to work out how to build the boat, and Fellows, Morton and Clayton gave him a present of £5 for doing it — a lot of money in those days.

167 A horsedrawn wide boat is pulled out of Denham Deep Lock, loaded with gravel, about 1920. The boat is likely to have just loaded at Harefield, so the men are cleaning down while a girl steers.

168

168 *Roger* and *Raymond* head
towards Denham Deep Lock
loaded with coal on their way to
the Jam Factory at Southall in
1968. The boats were operated by
Blue Line Canal Carriers, who had
taken them over when Samuel
Barlow's finished carrying. This
particular traffic finished permanently soon after.

Index

Acknowledgements

In the course of research for this book, I have received help from a great number of people throughout England. It would be impossible to mention them all, but the omission of their names does not render my thanks any the less sincere.

In particular, I should like to thank Graham Diprose for his help in copying a large proportion of the photographs that comprise this book, and for the use of his dark room; David and Joyce Gladwin of the Waterways Research Centre for their advice and encouragement; Mrs Judy Kelnor for typing most of the manuscipt; Sally Mason for assistance with indexing; Tam and Di Murrell for a useful lead; Miss Fiona Marsden, Curator of the Sussex Archaeological Society; Mr James Howson of Dagenham Library; Mr John Epton, Secretary of the Thames and Medway Canal Association; Tony London, Curator of the Waterways Museum, Stoke Bruerne; Mr T. J. Penfold of H. Sabey & Co Ltd; Tony Harmsworth; Mr R. Brown, librarian to the Port of London Authority; Miss M. Swarbrick of the Victoria Library; and the staff of Chiswick Library.

I would like to thank the following for permission to reproduce copyright illustrations: Hammersmith Library: 1; The Radio Times Hulton Picture Library: *frontis*, 2, 32, 106, 109, 117-20, 133, 137, 156; Victoria and Albert Museum: 3; Chiswick Public Library: 5-10, 144, 147-9, 158; D. D. and J. M. Gladwin: 51; Dartford Public Library: 12-15; Gravesend Public Library: 16, 20-1; Thames and Medway Canal Association: 17-19; Eastgate Museum, Rochester: 22-3; Springfield County Library, Maidstone: 24-7; South-Eastern Newspapers Ltd: 28-31, 33; Tonbridge Historical Society: 34-5; Hastings Public Library: 36, 40-1; Sussex Archaeological Society: 37-9, 42; Reeves Collection (reproduced by courtesy of the *Sunday Times* and the Sussex Archaeological Society): 43; Dr Edwin Course: 44; Winchester City Museum: 45; Chichester Museum: 46; Littlehampton Museum: 47-8; Brighton Library: 49; Wey and Arun Canal Society: 52; Guildford Museum: 53-5, 57, 60, 66; Helen and Keith Tagg: 58; Weybridge Library: 61-5; The Harmsworth Family Collection: 67-71; Hampshire County Museum Service: 72; Mr A. Gostelow: 73-5; Port of London Authority: 76-9; Museum of London: 80-1; Walworth Road Library, Southwark Collection: 82-3; Public Record Office/British Railways Board: 84-7; Victoria Public Library: 88-94; Mr S. Murdoch: 95; Dagenham Library: 96, 98-100; R. Sida: 97; Hertford Museum: 101-3; British Waterways Board, Waterways Museum: 104, 107, 112-16, 131-2, 134-6, 151-2, 160-2; Cheshunt Library: 105; Pickfords Ltd: 123, 126; *Daily Herald* Collection: 125, 129, 138, 159; Cyril Arapoff Collection: 128, 130, 150; H. Sabey Ltd: 139-40; Wembley Historical Society: 141; Ealing Public Library: 142; Kensington Public Library: 143; Topix: 154; *The Times* Picture Library: 155, 157; Southall District Library: 163-4; Middlesex County Press: 165-6; Hillingdon Central Library: 167; The following photographs are from my own collection: 4, 11, 50, 56, 59, 108, 110, 111, 124, 168.